REGENTS RESTORATION DRAMA SERIES

General Editor: John Loftis

THE MAN OF MODE

GEORGE ETHEREGE

The Man of Mode

Edited by

W. B. CARNOCHAN

UNIVERSITY OF NEBRASKA PRESS · LINCOLN

Publishers on the Plains

UNP

60102

Regents Restoration Drama Series

The Regents Restoration Drama Series, similar in objectives and format to the Regents Renaissance Drama Series, will provide soundly edited texts, in modern spelling, of the more significant English plays of the late seventeenth and early eighteenth centuries. The word "Restoration" is here used ambiguously and must be explained. If to the historian it refers to the period between 1660 and 1685 (or 1688), it has long been used by the student of drama in default of a more precise word to refer to plays belonging to the dramatic tradition established in the 1660's, weakening after 1700, and displaced in the 1730's. It is in this extended sense—imprecise though justified by academic custom—that the word is used in this series, which will include plays first produced between 1660 and 1737. Although these limiting dates are determined by political events, the return of Charles II (and the removal of prohibitions against the operation of theaters) and the passage of Walpole's Stage Licensing Act, they enclose a period of dramatic history having a coherence of its own in the establishment, development, and disintegration of a tradition.

Each text in the series is based on a fresh collation of the seventeenth- and eighteenth-century editions that might be presumed to have authority. The textual notes, which appear above the rule at the bottom of each page, record all substantive departures from the edition used as the copy-text. Variant substantive readings among contemporary editions are listed there as well. Editions later than the eighteenth century are referred to in the textual notes only when an emendation originating in some one of them is received into the text. Variants of accidentals (spelling, punctuation, capitalization) are not recorded in the notes. Contracted forms of characters' names are silently expanded in speech prefixes and stage directions, and, in the case of speech prefixes, are regularized. Additions to the stage directions of the copy-text are enclosed in brackets. Stage directions such as "within" or "aside" are enclosed in parentheses when they occur in the copy-text.

Spelling has been modernized along consciously conservative lines, but within the limits of a modernized text the linguistic quality of the original has been carefully preserved. Contracted preterites have regularly been expanded. Punctuation has been brought into accord with modern practices. The objective has been to achieve a balance between the pointing of the old editions and a system of punctuation which, without overloading the text with exclamation marks, semicolons, and dashes, will make the often loosely flowing verse and prose of the original syntactically intelligible to the modern reader. Dashes are regularly used only to indicate interrupted speeches, or shifts of address within a single speech.

Explanatory notes, chiefly concerned with glossing obsolete words and phrases, are printed below the textual notes at the bottom of each page. References to stage directions in the notes follow the admirable system of the Revels editions, whereby stage directions are keyed, decimally, to the line of the text before or after which they occur. Thus, a note on 0.2 has reference to the second line of the stage direction at the beginning of the scene in question. A note on 115.1 has reference to the first line of the stage direction following line 115 of the text of the relevant scene. Speech prefixes, and any stage directions attached to them, are keyed to the first line of accompanying dialogue.

JOHN LOFTIS

Stanford University

Contents

List of Abbreviations

Brett-Smith	H. F. B. Brett-Smith, ed. *The Dramatic Works of Sir George Etherege*. 2 vols. Oxford, 1927.
CBEP	*The Man of Mode*, in Vol. VI of *A Collection of the Best English Plays*. London, [1711?]. Octavo.
D	*The Man of Mode*, 1733. Duodecimo.
MacMillan-Jones	Dougald MacMillan and Howard Mumford Jones, eds. *Plays of the Restoration and Eighteenth Century*. New York,'1931.
MLN	*Modern Language Notes*
Nettleton-Case	George H. Nettleton and Arthur E. Case, eds. *British Dramatists from Dryden to Sheridan*. Cambridge, Mass., 1939.
O	*The Man of Mode*, 1711. Octavo.
OED	*Oxford English Dictionary*
Q1	*The Man of Mode*, 1676. Quarto.
Q2	*The Man of Mode*, 1684. Quarto.
Q3	*The Man of Mode*, 1693. Quarto.
RES	*Review of English Studies*
S.D.	stage direction
Thorn Drury	G. Thorn Drury, ed. *The Poems of Edmund Waller*. 2 vols. London: The Muses' Library.
Tilley	Morris Palmer Tilley. *A Dictionary of the Proverbs in England in the Sixteenth and Seventeenth Centuries*. Ann Arbor, 1950.
Verity	A. Wilson Verity, ed. *The Works of Sir George Etheredge*. London, 1888.
1704	*The Works of Sir George Etherege*. London, 1704. Octavo.

Introduction

The last of Etherege's three plays, *The Man of Mode* was licensed for publication on June 3, 1676, and entered in the Stationers' Register on June 15: "a book or copy intituled *The Man of mode or, Sir Fopling Flutter* a comoedy, written by George Etheridge, Esqr." [1] It is unlikely that Etherege supervised the publication. The first edition (Q1) is carelessly printed, but it is more reliable than any other of the early editions. Etherege surely played no part in the publication of a quarto of 1684 (Q2), which introduces new errors. A quarto of 1693 (Q3), two years after Etherege's death, closely follows Q2; and the text in the collected works of 1704, though based on Q1, is corrupt in additional details. The present modernized edition uses Q1 as the copy-text and is based on a collation of Q1–3 and 1704. [2] In cases of special interest, variants are recorded from later editions in the textual notes. All editions of the play through 1733 and all collected editions of Etherege have been consulted.

The play presents a problem in modernization because of its erratic and inaccurate use of accent marks on French words and phrases in the early editions. Modern editors have sometimes thought that forms such as *coquetté* for *coquette* indicate mispronunciations by Sir Fopling. No clear pattern exists, however, and the problems of accentuation in *The Man of Mode* are not unique: in early editions of Etherege's *The Comical Revenge* (1664), as in Wycherley's *The Gentleman Dancing Master* (1673), almost indiscriminate accents, especially on final *e*'s, mark both French and English when spoken with a French accent. In the present text, the French has been corrected and modernized throughout. [3]

---

[1] *A Transcript of the Register of the Worshipful Company of Stationers; From 1640–1708 A.D.* (London, 1913), III, 22.

[2] Donald Wing, *Short Title Catalogue* (New York, 1945) lists an edition of 1697 (E3377). I have found no other record of it nor any evidence for its existence.

[3] If Sir Fopling's French is lame, he becomes a character of farce—not, as Dryden calls him in the Epilogue, "a fool so nicely writ,/ The ladies would mistake him for a wit." His accent, appropriate to a character who

The earliest recorded performance—and perhaps the first—was that at the Duke's Theatre in Dorset Garden on March 11, 1676.[4] It had been eight years since Etherege's last play. The King's presence at this performance and at another the next month reflects the literary and social importance attached to *The Man of Mode*. Thomas Betterton, the most famous actor of the age, played Dorimant; Mrs. Barry, beginning a career that would rival Betterton's, may have played Mrs. Loveit[5]—a part that took precedence over Harriet's throughout the stage history of the play. Other roles went to other leading members of the company, and special care was taken with the costumes. Sir Car Scroope, poet and courtier, had written the prologue; John Dryden, the epilogue. The success of *The Man of Mode*, both immediate and "extraordinary,"[6] was appropriate to the glitter that surrounded its first appearance.

Though stage records are fragmentary for the seventeenth century, the continuing popularity of the play is beyond question. A friend of Etherege, writing him in December, 1685, tells of a performance at court that was received with "the usual applause."[7] This popularity survived well into the eighteenth century. In the words of Richard Steele, writing in *The Spectator*, No. 65, May 15, 1711: "The received opinion of this play is, that it is the pattern of genteel comedy." Not until the 1730's was there any decline in its drawing power: in the years 1710–1720, for example, performances are recorded on the average of three a year, and there were at least as many over the next decade. Among those who played roles were Colley Cibber as Sir Fopling; Mrs. Oldfield as Mrs. Loveit; Mrs. Bracegirdle as Harriet; Robert Wilks as Dorimant; William Pinkethman as Old Bellair. After 1730 the play was produced less frequently for the next two decades, some-

---

is all form and no substance, may well be perfect, despite the obvious limits to his knowledge of Parisian life.

[4] "His Ma^ts Bill from His Royall Highnesse Theatre," dated June 29, 1677. P.R.O., L.C. 5/142, p. 81 (quoted in Allardyce Nicoll, *A History of Restoration Drama, 1660–1700*, 4th edn. [Cambridge, 1952], p. 348).

[5] Mrs. Barry is listed for the part by John Downes, *Roscius Anglicanus* (London, 1708), p. 36. John Harold Wilson thinks it likely that the role was created by Mary Lee and inherited by Mrs. Barry after Mrs. Lee's retirement in 1685 (*All the King's Ladies* [Chicago, 1958], p. 111).

[6] [Charles Gildon], *The Lives and Characters of the English Dramatick Poets* (London, 1699[?]), p. 53.

[7] Charles, Earl of Middleton, to Etherege, December 7, 1685. *The Letter-book of Sir George Etherege*, ed. Sybil Rosenfeld (London, 1928), p. 345.

times with Theophilus Cibber succeeding his father as Sir Fopling. But *The Man of Mode* had by now had its day. A performance of October, 1755, was "much disliked and hissed." In the next twenty years, only one revival is recorded.[8] A 1965 revival at the Georgian Theatre, Richmond, Yorkshire, was announced as the first since 1793.

Etherege's portrait of Sir Fopling raises in miniature a traditional question about the ancestry of Restoration drama—whether it is mainly French or English; in the case of comedy, whether it derives mainly from the models of Ben Jonson, Beaumont and Fletcher, and John Shirley, or from Molière. The question, in *The Man of Mode*, turns on the relationship of Sir Fopling to Mascarille, the masquerading valet of Molière's *Les Précieuses Ridicules*. Scholarship has recently discounted or minimized the importance of Molière for Restoration drama;[9] the case of *The Man of Mode* affirms that verdict. Mascarille pretends to be a fop, Sir Fopling is one; though they share foppish traits, and though Etherege, perhaps, remembers Mascarille in a general way, specific borrowing, if any, is limited to one instance—Sir Fopling's roll call of his servants.[10] There is little evidence to prove a significant debt.

In any event *The Man of Mode* cannot be classed as a "derivative" play. It is of its own time and place—so much so that, according to John Dennis, it was believed to be "an agreeable Representation of the Persons of Condition of both Sexes, both in Court and Town."[11] Dorimant—amorous, inconstant, and forever quoting Waller—was taken for the Earl of Rochester; Medley, says Dennis, was modeled on Sir Fleetwood Sheppard; and Sir Fopling has traditionally been identified as the notorious fop Beau Hewitt. These identifications, even that of Dorimant, are in fact speculative. At one time or another, Dorimant, Medley, and Young Bellair have each been taken for

[8] For the stage history of the play in the seventeenth and eighteenth centuries, see *The London Stage*, ed. William Van Lennep, Emmett L. Avery, Arthur H. Scouten, George Winchester Stone, Jr., and Charles Beecher Hogan (Carbondale, Illinois, 1960–   ).

[9] See, for example, John Wilcox, *The Relation of Molière to Restoration Comedy* (New York, 1938).

[10] See Arthur Sherbo, "A Note on *The Man of Mode*," *MLN*, LXIV (May, 1949), 343–344.

[11] *The Critical Works of John Dennis*, ed. Edward Niles Hooker (Baltimore, 1939, 1943), II, 248.

Etherege's self-portrait. In name and character, Medley recalls Sir Charles Sedley. The tradition that links Sir Fopling and Beau Hewitt is also suspect: though a dandy, Hewitt was not at all the same sort of precious fool as Sir Fopling.[12] Dryden, in the Epilogue, invokes the satirist's usual claim that the individual has been spared: ". . .none Sir Fopling him, or him, can call:/ He's knight o' th' shire and represents ye all." For once, the claim is probably just. Details, or suggestive hints, of individual portraiture merge in the picture of a society. That society, dazzled by the picture, understandably looked for and thought it found more precise reflections of its own image.

Etherege's earlier plays—*The Comical Revenge* (1664) and *She Would if She Could* (1668)—had tested and refined the comic possibilities of Restoration life as he saw and experienced it. Each play is apprentice work for *The Man of Mode*. *The Comical Revenge* moves uneasily between farce and rhymed heroics; yet in its comic moments, as H. F. B. Brett-Smith has said, its audiences "were suddenly confronted with the world they knew."[13] *She Would if She Could* turns away from rhyme and, for the courtly themes of love and honor, substitutes the comic metaphor of the love duel in which wit and high seriousness are closely mingled. With *She Would if She Could*, says Brett-Smith, "the new comedy of manners has come to its own."[14] And, with *The Man of Mode*, the new comedy is in full flower.

Here are the love duel, the fop, the libertine, the conflict between generations, the oppositions of country and town, of England and France—in short, almost all the themes and characters that we associate with the tradition of Restoration comedy. Etherege's treatment of character, in particular, sets a standard of precision and delicate nuance by which to measure the tradition as a whole. Sir Fopling assimilates the stock figure of the affected Frenchman or Francophile and, at the same time, sets the type for a more indigenous breed of fops such as Vanbrugh's Lord Foppington—a line that stretches into the eighteenth century. Dorimant has only one rival—Horner, of *The Country Wife* (1675), with whom he shares a common ancestry in the satyr-satirist of Renaissance drama—as the most formidable libertine of the age. Harriet has only one rival—Millamant, of *The Way of the*

[12] See Arthur Sherbo, "Sir Fopling Flutter and Beau Hewitt," *Notes and Queries*, CXIV (July, 1949), 296–303.

[13] H. F. B. Brett-Smith, ed., *The Dramatic Works of Sir George Etherege* (Oxford, 1927), p. lxxiii.

[14] *Ibid.*, p. lxxvii.

World (1700)—as the most engaging heroine in the wars of love. Sir Fopling, Dorimant, and Harriet claim our attention equally. None triumphs as a dramatic character at the expense of another. It is to them, especially, that *The Man of Mode* owes its representative quality. As "the pattern of genteel comedy," the play has borne the burden of acute moral indignation ever since the eighteenth century. Steele called it, in *The Spectator*, No. 65, "a perfect contradiction to good manners, good sense, and common honesty." That it took longer for Steele's opinion to prevail than the schematizations of literary history might suggest is clear from the stage history of *The Man of Mode*; but its virtual disappearance from the stage by the mid-century—coinciding with the extraordinary popularity of Steele's *The Conscious Lovers*—marks the triumph of sentiment in comedy, a triumph with effects that have never been quite undone. Even in this century, Montague Summers called *The Man of Mode* "the most immoral comedy I know."[15]

Critics such as John Dennis have defended Etherege's play—and, by implication, Restoration comedy—on the grounds of its satiric content. Critics such as Charles Lamb, taking a different line, have defended Restoration comedy on the grounds that it gives us only a fantasy world in which moral concerns are irrelevant. The satiric intent of *The Man of Mode*, in the crucial case of Dorimant, needs demonstration; and the libertine hero still offends conventional morality, no matter what may be the relationship between fiction and historical fact. On our view of Dorimant, our sense of the play's moral structure must largely depend.

Certainly it is hard to see *The Man of Mode* as the completed comedy of a redeemed rake. Though Dorimant (we may assume) follows Harriet to the country at the close, he assures Mrs. Loveit that his motives are financial; and he leaves some open possibilities in town—or would like to. He tells Bellinda, the mistress he has most recently played false, "We must meet again":

BELLINDA.
    Never.
DORIMANT.
    Never?   (V.ii.280–282)

Despite Bellinda's subsequent harsh answer, some readers, like Dorimant, have assessed his chances more hopefully. Etherege does not

[15] *The Playhouse of Pepys* (London, 1935), p. 312.

firmly tie the cord that binds the penitent rake within the institutions of society. Why, then, this uncertain ending?

The answer lies in the complexities of Dorimant's character. As the play opens, we see him at leisure and "unmasked"; the first act is his, the revelation of his private character. It sets up echoes that sound through the play and serve as comment on public actions. Specifically, it shows Dorimant as an impulsive libertine and, at the same time, a "good-natured" man. He complains in his first lines that he has paid "a tax upon good nature" in the billet-doux he has written Mrs. Loveit "after the heat of the business is over" (I.i.4–5). On the one hand, conventional good nature demands that pretenses, for a time, be kept up; on the other, good nature is linked with impulse and the tax unwillingly paid. Later in the play, impulse will jar increasingly against the obligations and mores of society: the tax that society puts on Dorimant's good nature becomes a main source of irony as his pursuit of self-gratification more and more requires him to abide by the rules of society's game. But the equation of good nature and impulse points at the start to what is most important in Dorimant's private character.

His treatment of the servants, which looks at first like indifference, can be construed as indulgence. He tells Handy to call a footman, but none answers:

DORIMANT.
    Dogs! Will they ever lie snoring abed till noon?
HANDY.
    'Tis all one, sir: if they're up, you indulge 'em so, they're ever poaching after whores all the morning.

                                            (I.i.16–18)

Complaisant with his own servants, Dorimant is equally so with the orange-woman and the shoemaker—each of them a minor triumph of genre art. He abuses them, of course, but not in the spirit of contempt; and they abuse him in turn. The verbal combats imply the equality of the participants: when Dorimant finally gives the orange-woman ten shillings for a basket of fruit (and on the chance that she can do him some service with Harriet), or when he pays the shoemaker half a crown with which to drink his health, payment is made for value rendered or expected. This should not obscure the good-natured impulse behind Dorimant's offhand manner. It is a long way from

Dorimant to Fielding's Tom Jones; it may not be wholly fanciful, however, to suppose a lineal relationship between them.

The alliance of libertine temperament and good nature seems to have been, for Etherege, a matter of personal concern. In letters from Ratisbon, where at the end of his life he spent several years as envoy, he paints his own self-portrait: "I need not tell you I am good-natured," he writes to a friend who had not answered an earlier letter; "I who have forgiven so many mistresses who have been false to me can well forgive a friend who has only been negligent. My heart was never touched for any for whom there remains not still some impression of kindness."[16] In another letter he writes of the "chastity" that age and circumstance have forced on him: "While we approach this virtue let us take care our years do not sour us with any of the common vices of age; let us still preserve our good humour and our good nature."[17] Etherege takes care to seem more sinned against than sinning—and so distinguishes himself from Dorimant. Yet Dorimant's behavior in the first act is designed as a mark of "that openness of heart and hand which," wrote Bishop Burnet, "sometimes makes a libertine so amiable."[18]

An incident at the close of the act confirms these early impressions of Dorimant and lets us see more clearly the satiric function of his role. A footman delivers a letter from a whore whom he has loved and left. He reads the letter—"I have no money and am very malicolly. Pray send me a guynie to see the operies" (I.i.470–471)—to his friend Medley:

MEDLEY.

Pray let the whore have a favorable answer, that she may spark it in a box and do honor to her profession.

DORIMANT.

She shall, and perk up i' the face of quality.

(I.i.473–475)

Medley is making fun of the whore; Dorimant proposes to make fun of "quality." He is the instrument, that is, of satire; his mode, in this case, is a burlesque of the fashionable world. As in *Tom Jones*, the

16 *The Letterbook of Sir George Etherege*, p. 206.

17 *Ibid.*, p. 283.

18 *Bishop Burnet's History of His Own Time*, quoted in *The Letterbook of Sir George Etherege*, p. 161 n.

scapegrace behavior of the good-natured man becomes a commentary on the forms and conventions of society.

In Dorimant's dressing room, as we learn much later from Sir Fopling, there is no mirror:

SIR FOPLING.

Prithee, Dorimant, why hast not thou a glass hung up here? A room is the dullest thing without one.

YOUNG BELLAIR.

Here is company to entertain you.

SIR FOPLING.

But I mean in case of being alone. In a glass a man may entertain himself—

DORIMANT.

The shadow of himself, indeed.   (IV.ii.83–88)

In the public world of the play, Dorimant is contrasted with those preoccupied with their looking-glasses: not Sir Fopling only—so fragile and perfect in his absurdity that criticism runs the risk of treading too close, or too heavily—but also Mrs. Loveit. Our first view of her is important. She comes on stage with her maid, sets aside a letter, then takes out her pocket glass: "I hate myself, I look so ill today" (II.ii.3). The mirror as emblem links Sir Fopling with Mrs. Loveit; and Dorimant, as satiric agent, creates a specific link between them. Seeking an excuse to break off with Loveit, he charges her with designing a conquest of Sir Fopling. The charge of course is untrue; but Loveit, in an effort to revenge herself by making Dorimant jealous, pretends emotions she does not feel and strikes up an alliance with Sir Fopling. The action reinforces the satiric point: very different as they are—the one passionate and violent, the other ridiculous and effete—Loveit and Sir Fopling are in one respect alike. Each is captive to the image in the glass, hence to a shadow of the self.

Dorimant points also to society's habitual veiling of its real self. He will "pluck off," so he says, the mask of Loveit's pretended passion for Sir Fopling "and show the passion that lies panting under" (III.iii.309–310). He scoffs at Sir Fopling, who appears uninvited with his servants, all of them masked, at Lady Townley's party.

DORIMANT.

What's here—masquerades?

HARRIET.

I thought that foppery had been left off, and people might have been in private with a fiddle.

DORIMANT.

'Tis endeavored to be kept on foot still by some who find
themselves the more acceptable, the less they are known.

(IV.i.169–174)

By now, however, Dorimant himself has become vulnerable, for he
is no longer what he was at first. In society, he is forced to shifts,
evasions, masquerades. Another in a long tradition of satirists sat-
irized, he has become the victim of Etherege's irony. Loveit's counterplot, after all, has had some success. It does make Dorimant
jealous, and he conceals his instinctive reaction: "I am concerned
but dare not show it" (III.iii.280–281). Dorimant cannot gain his
ends—in this case the conquest of Bellinda—without dissembling.
And the scene at Lady Townley's confirms our sense of his ambivalent
position: at the moment when he makes fun of Sir Fopling and
his maskers, he is in masquerade himself; in order to trick Lady
Woodvill, whose fear of him amounts almost to monomania, he
has passed himself off as "Mr. Courtage"—"that foppish admirer
of quality, who flatters the very meat at honorable tables and
never offers love to a woman below a lady-grandmother" (III.iii.323–
325). What he says of Sir Fopling is more nearly true of himself:
Dorimant is the more acceptable the less he is known; Sir Fopling,
unmasked, is accepted by all the company. Dorimant's stratagem
reminds us that he, as well as Sir Fopling, is a man of mode.
Etherege's tactics here are those of satiric reversal, and he enforces
his point by letting Sir Fopling parody the role of unmasker: in his
simple-mindedness, Sir Fopling forgets that Dorimant, for the
moment, is not Dorimant at all and twice blurts out "Courtage's"
real name. Dorimant's part is to laugh at affectation but also to be
laughed at; he too participates in society's self-disguise.

A dialogue between Harriet and Young Bellair reflects the
double view of Dorimant that emerges from the action. They talk of
him:

HARRIET.

He's agreeable and pleasant, I must own, but he does so
much affect being so, he displeases me.

YOUNG BELLAIR.

Lord, madam, all he does and says is so easy and so natural.

HARRIET.

Some men's verses seem so to the unskilful; but labor i' the

one and affectation in the other to the judicious plainly
appear.

YOUNG BELLAIR.

I never heard him accused of affectation before.

(III.iii.23–29)

Each is half right; or, to put it another way, each gives an accurate
account of one side of Dorimant's nature, divided as it is between the
world of private impulse and that of public deceptions.

The division between these worlds is, however, artificial in the long
run: private impulses lead to public actions and raise public questions
of morality. In the last act of the play, Etherege maintains the double
view of Dorimant at the cost of a wholly consistent mood. Lady
Woodvill's miraculous conversion and Loveit's utter humiliation are
in one light the expected rewards of Dorimant's good nature and
resourcefulness. But earlier in the act he appears in quite another
light as a comic intriguer caught up and revealed in his own intrigues. When Bellinda surprises him by accident at Mrs. Loveit's, he
admits that "I never was at such a loss before" (V.i.256). When
Bellinda and Loveit appear together at Lady Townley's in the final
scene, his embarrassment is acute: "The devil owes me a shame
today, and I think never will have done paying it" (V.ii.225–226).
What Dorimant feels as social embarrassment, we feel as an implied
moral judgment. The colloquial identification of Dorimant, throughout the play, as an "arrant devil" (I.i.108) or "the prince of all the
devils in the town" (III.iii.111–112) or, in Loveit's view, a devil with
"something of the angel yet undefaced in him" (II.ii.15–16) achieves
in its persistence a more than colloquial force. When Dorimant
acknowledges, in the proverbial phrase, that the devil owes him a
shame, we almost expect him to be laughed and hissed from the stage.

But not so. The direction of events is reversed; Mrs. Loveit is con-
signed to the darkness of her own tormented spirit; Dorimant and
Harriet triumph in her defeat. Will events prove, however, as
Dorimant protests to Harriet, that "this day my soul has quite given
up her liberty" (V.ii.386–387)? If Dorimant were to put on peniten-
tial robes and pair off in the usual way with Harriet, he would seem
to compromise the claims of impulse. Yet traditional morality has
also made its claims. The tentative nature of the ending is determined
by the alternative views of Dorimant proposed in the play.

We need not guess at events beyond the conclusion to recognize a logic that could resolve the dilemma; for Harriet offers Dorimant a chance to reconcile nature and art. Like him she scorns the mirror of fashion, and her third act entrance is contrasted, specifically, with Mrs. Loveit's entrance in the last scene of Act II. Impulsively, Harriet has just walked out on her mother and on Young Bellair, intended for her husband:

BUSY.
  Dear madam, let me set that curl in order.
HARRIET.
  Let me alone, I will shake 'em all out of order!

(III.i.1–2)

Harriet will have nothing to do with society's "powdering," "painting," and "patching" (III.i.15); and, like Dorimant again, she is a satiric commentator on social affectations. Her typical weapon is parody: with Young Bellair she pantomimes the gestures of conventional lovers, and she mimics Dorimant in his role as gallant. But, unlike Dorimant, she is safe from irony. Though she sometimes goes masked, and in this way gets her chance to watch Dorimant as he flirts with another woman, yet she makes no compromises; masked or unmasked, she is the same. That is to say, she is free; Dorimant, though he does not know it, has partially surrendered his liberty in the adjustments he makes to realize his desires. If Harriet's "pleasing image" has settled in his "soul" (III.iii.122–123), the Christian paradox is realized: in her service is the possibility of freedom.

The pervasive religious imagery of the play carries a special burden of meaning.[19] Near the end, Harriet expresses her doubts in Dorimant's good faith, and he reassures her: "The prospect of such a heav'n will make me persevere and give you marks that are infallible" (V.ii.132–133). But when Dorimant pledges a monkish asceticism and promises, with a witty merging of religious and economic images, to "sacrifice to you all the interest I have in other women," Harriet stops him: "Hold! Though I wish you devout, I would not have you turn fanatic" (V.ii.136–138). Nor will she make vows to Dorimant, for "what we do then is expected from us and wants much of the welcome it finds when it surprises" (V.ii.150–151). Quite unlike Mrs. Loveit, a fanatic in love who exacts as many vows as she can, Harriet abridges neither her freedom nor Dorimant's with the tyranny of oaths

---

[19] On this subject, see Dale Underwood's valuable study, *Etherege and the Seventeenth-Century Comedy of Manners* (New Haven, 1957), p. 105 f.

and covenants. Whatever is given will be given freely, or not at all.

The alternative choices for Dorimant are clear enough: the continued accommodation of private desires through public masquerades or the freedom gained by a willing renunciation. The usual resolutions of comic plots lead us to expect the latter; and we may well be uneasy with the ending—such is the strength of normal expectations—even though it follows as the logical consequence of Dorimant's double role.

We may be uneasy, too, with the apparent shapelessness of Etherege's plot—as was that seventeenth-century critic who chided Etherege for thinking that "A Plot's too gross for any Play."[20] Certainly the shape of *The Man of Mode* is not that which comedy usually imposes. Rather, it is defined by confrontations of character, by thematic contrasts, and above all by patterns of verbal allusion and wit. The repeated images of love and sexual pursuit as religious experience, as gaming, as a business venture, lend weight to the puns and proverbs and colloquial rhythms of the dialogue. When Harriet asks Dorimant if he can "keep a Lent for a mistress" and Dorimant answers, "In expectation of a happy Easter" (III.iii.79–81), the sexual joke mirrors ironic themes of the fall, of grace, of redemption, that are at the heart of the play.[21] Often the images work in less conspicuous ways. Young Bellair, for example, warns Dorimant not to hope for Harriet on any terms but marriage: "Without church security, there's no taking up there" (IV.ii.179–180). At first the metaphor is scarcely felt. "Security" might be merely an abstraction; "taking up" has a usual meaning of "setting up house" and easily suggests a bawdy pun. But the commercial metaphor—in which "taking up" means "borrowing at interest"—emerges from the background; and, as in Dorimant's pledge that he will sacrifice to Harriet all his interest in other women, the commercial and the religious come together ("church security") to qualify and deepen a first response. On such effects of wit and compression the verbal temper and, finally, the unity of *The Man of Mode* depend. Even so, the absence of conventional "plot" combines with the uncertain ending to balance the play, precariously, between the order of comedy and the disorder of things as they are.

[20] Alexander Radcliffe, "News from Hell," in *The Ramble* (London, 1682), p. 5.
[21] Underwood, *Etherege and the Seventeenth-Century Comedy of Manners*, p. 106.

Yet *The Man of Mode* overcomes critical doubts—by the range and skill of its portraiture, by its wit and grace, and ultimately by its good nature. The memory of Mrs. Loveit's destruction fades and it is Harriet we remember, as she challenges Dorimant to follow her to the "great, rambling, lone house" (V.ii.379) in the country, then laughs at his solemn declarations and at herself: "This is more dismal than the country.—Emilia, pity me who am going to that sad place. Methinks I hear the hateful noise of rooks already—kaw, kaw, kaw. There's music in the worst cry in London. 'My dill and cucumbers to pickle'" (V.ii.388–391). Her voice merges with the sounds of country and town; the fiddles strike up for the last dance; and the effect is of a final harmony, no matter how much, in fact, remains to be played.

I am grateful to the William Andrews Clark Memorial Library, University of California, Los Angeles, for a summer fellowship that enabled me to finish this edition; and to the staff of the Clark Library for generous help.

W. B. CARNOCHAN

Stanford University

THE MAN OF MODE

To Her Royal Highness
The Duchess

MADAM,

Poets, however they may be modest otherwise, have
always too good an opinion of what they write. The world,
when it sees this play dedicated to your Royal Highness, will
conclude I have more than my share of that vanity. But I   5
hope the honor I have of belonging to you will excuse my
presumption. 'Tis the first thing I have produced in your
service, and my duty obliges me to what my choice durst not
else have aspired.

I am very sensible, madam, how much it is beholding to   10
your indulgence for the success it had in the acting, and
your protection will be no less fortunate to it in the printing;
for all are so ambitious of making their court to you that
none can be severe to what you are pleased to favor.

This universal submission and respect is due to the great-   15
ness of your rank and birth; but you have other illustrious
qualities which are much more engaging. Those would but
dazzle, did not these really charm the eyes and understand-
ings of all who have the happiness to approach you.

Authors on these occasions are never wanting to publish a   20
particular of their patron's virtues and perfections; but your
Royal Highness's are so eminently known that, did I follow
their examples, I should but paint those wonders here of
which everyone already has the idea in his mind. Besides, I
do not think it proper to aim at that in prose which is so   25
glorious a subject for verse, in which hereafter if I show
more zeal than skill, it will not grieve me much, since I less
passionately desire to be esteemed a poet than to be
thought,

                    Madam,   30
               Your Royal Highness's
             most humble, most obedient,
                and most faithful servant,
                         GEORGE ETHEREGE

10. beholding] *Q 1–2, 1704;* be-
holden *Q 3.*

Her . . . Duchess] Mary of Modena, Duchess of York (1658–1718).

8. *service*] Of Etherege's "service" to the Duchess of York, nothing is
known. The Duke of York granted Etherege a pension in 1682 and, as
James II, sent him as envoy to Ratisbon in 1685.

PROLOGUE

By Sir Car Scroope, Baronet

Like dancers on the ropes poor poets fare:
Most perish young, the rest in danger are.
This, one would think, should make our authors wary,
But, gamester-like, the giddy fools miscarry;
A lucky hand or two so tempts 'em on,   5
They cannot leave off play till they're undone.
With modest fears a muse does first begin,
Like a young wench newly enticed to sin;
But tickled once with praise, by her good will,
The wanton fool would never more lie still.   10
'Tis an old mistress you'll meet here tonight,
Whose charms you once have looked on with delight.
But now, of late, such dirty drabs have known ye,
A muse o'th' better sort's ashamed to own ye.
Nature well-drawn and wit must now give place   15
To gaudy nonsense and to dull grimace;
Nor is it strange that you should like so much
That kind of wit, for most of yours is such.
But I'm afraid that while to France we go,   ⎫
To bring you home fine dresses, dance, and show, ⎬   20
The stage, like you, will but more foppish grow. ⎭
Of foreign wares why should we fetch the scum,
When we can be so richly served at home?
For, heav'n be thanked, 'tis not so wise an age
But your own follies may supply the stage.   25
Though often plowed, there's no great fear the soil
Should barren grow by the too-frequent toil,
While at your doors are to be daily found
Such loads of dunghill to manure the ground.
'Tis by your follies that we players thrive,   30

6. off] *Q1, Q3, 1704;* of *Q2.*   14. ye] *Q2–3;* you *Q1, 1704.*
11. mistress] *Q3, 1704; Q1–2 print*
Mrs.

Sir Car Scroope] poet and courtier (1649–1680).
9. *will*] with a pun on *Will* as a proper name.
13. *drabs*] sluts.

As the physicians by diseases live;
And as each year some new distemper reigns,
Whose friendly poison helps t'increase their gains,
So, among you, there starts up every day
Some new, unheard-of fool for us to play.   35
Then, for your own sakes, be not too severe,
Nor what you all admire at home, damn here.
Since each is fond of his own ugly face,
Why should you, when we hold it, break the glass?

33. t'increase] *Q 2–3, 1704;* to increase *Q 1.*

DRAMATIS PERSONAE

MR. DORIMANT ⎫
MR. MEDLEY, [his friend] ⎪
OLD BELLAIR ⎬ Gentlemen
YOUNG BELLAIR, [his son, in love with Emilia] ⎪
SIR FOPLING FLUTTER ⎭ 5

LADY TOWNLEY, [sister of Old Bellair] ⎫
EMILIA ⎪
MRS. LOVEIT, [in love with Dorimant] ⎪
BELLINDA, [in love with Dorimant] ⎬ Gentlewomen
LADY WOODVILL, and ⎪ 10
HARRIET, her daughter ⎭

PERT ⎫
and ⎬ Waiting women
BUSY ⎭

A SHOEMAKER 15
AN ORANGE-WOMAN
THREE SLOVENLY BULLIES
TWO CHAIRMEN
MR. SMIRK, a parson
HANDY, a valet de chambre 20
PAGES. FOOTMEN, etc.

The Man of Mode

or,

Sir Fopling Flutter

A Comedy

ACT I

A dressing room. A table covered with a toilet; clothes laid ready. Enter Dorimant *in his gown and slippers, with a note in his hand made up, repeating verses.*

DORIMANT.

"Now, for some ages, had the pride of Spain
Made the sun shine on half the world in vain."

Then looking on the note.

"For Mrs. Loveit." What a dull, insipid thing is a billet-doux written in cold blood, after the heat of the business is over! It is a tax upon good nature which I have here been   5
laboring to pay, and have done it, but with as much regret as ever fanatic paid the Royal Aid or church duties. 'Twill have

---

3. "For Mrs. Loveit."] *For Mrs. Loveit Q 1–3, 1704. MacMillan-Jones and Nettleton-Case print as here. Verity prints as a continuation of the*

S.D. The intention of the early editions is ambiguous because of the italic type and the location of the phrase on the printed page.

0.1. *toilet*] cloth cover, probably of rich material.
0.2. *made up*] To "make up" a letter is usually to close and seal it; but see I.i.177 f.
1–2. *Now . . . vain*] Waller, "Of a War with Spain, and a Fight at Sea," ll. 1–2 (Thorn Drury, II, 23).
7. *fanatic*] one opposed to the religious and civil establishment; a dissenter.
7. *Royal Aid*] tax levied by parliament on behalf of the King.
7. *church duties*] local duties charged for services of the parish church.

the same fate, I know, that all my notes to her have had of late; 'twill not be thought kind enough. Faith, women are i' the right when they jealously examine our letters, for in 10 them we always first discover our decay of passion.—Hey! Who waits?

Enter Handy.

HANDY.

Sir—

DORIMANT.

Call a footman.

HANDY.

None of 'em are come yet.   15

DORIMANT.

Dogs! Will they ever lie snoring abed till noon?

HANDY.

'Tis all one, sir: if they're up, you indulge 'em so, they're ever poaching after whores all the morning.

DORIMANT.

Take notice henceforward who's wanting in his duty; the next clap he gets, he shall rot for an example. What vermin 20 are those chattering without?

HANDY.

Foggy Nan, the orange-woman, and swearing Tom, the shoemaker.

DORIMANT.

Go, call in that overgrown jade with the flasket of guts before her. Fruit is refreshing in a morning.   25

Exit Handy.

"It is not that I love you less,
    Than when before your feet I lay—"

Enter Orange-Woman [*and* Handy].

How now, double-tripe, what news do you bring?

ORANGE-WOMAN.

News! Here's the best fruit has come to town t' year. Gad,

10. the] *Q1–2, 1704;* th' *Q3.*   19. in his] *Q1–2, 1704;* in's *Q3.*

---

22. *Foggy*] fat, gross.   24. *flasket*] basket, tub.
26–27. *It . . . lay*] Waller, "The Self-Banished," ll. 1–2 (Thorn Drury, I, 101).

I was up before four o'clock this morning and bought all the   30
choice i' the market.

DORIMANT.

The nasty refuse of your shop.

ORANGE-WOMAN.

You need not make mouths at it. I assure you, 'tis all culled
ware.

DORIMANT.

The citizens buy better on a holiday in their walk to   35
Totnam.

ORANGE-WOMAN.

Good or bad, 'tis all one; I never knew you commend anything. Lord, would the ladies had heard you talk of 'em as I
have done.

Sets down the fruit.

Here, bid your man give me an angel.   40

DORIMANT [*to* Handy].

Give the bawd her fruit again.

ORANGE-WOMAN.

Well, on my conscience, there never was the like of you.—
God's my life, I had almost forgot to tell you, there is a
young gentlewoman, lately come to town with her mother,
that is so taken with you.   45

DORIMANT.

Is she handsome?

ORANGE-WOMAN.

Nay, gad, there are few finer women, I tell you but so, and a
hugeous fortune, they say. Here, eat this peach, it comes
from the stone; 'tis better than any Newington y' have
tasted.   50

38. 'em] *Q 1–2, 1704;* them *Q 3.*

---

35. *citizens*] tradespeople.
36. *Totnam*] Tottenham, an unfashionable northern suburb of London.
40. *angel*] gold coin worth ten shillings.
47. *Nay*] The interjection does not imply negation.
48–49. *it . . . stone*] The meaning is obscure. Nettleton-Case suggests that
the peach may be a freestone, a variety in which the flesh, when ripe, parts
freely from the stone.
49. *Newington*] town in Kent from which some varieties of peach took
their name.

DORIMANT (*taking the peach*).

This fine woman, I'll lay my life, is some awkward, ill-
fashioned country toad, who, not having above four dozen
of black hairs on her head, has adorned her baldness with a
large white fruz, that she may look sparkishly in the fore-
front of the King's box at an old play.   55

ORANGE-WOMAN.

Gad, you'd change your note quickly if you did but see
her!

DORIMANT.

How came she to know me?

ORANGE-WOMAN.

She saw you yesterday at the Change. She told me you
came and fooled with the woman at the next shop.   60

DORIMANT.

I remember, there was a mask observed me, indeed.
Fooled, did she say?

ORANGE-WOMAN.

Ay; I vow she told me twenty things you said too, and acted
with her head and with her body so like you—

Enter Medley.

MEDLEY.

Dorimant, my life, my joy, my darling sin! How dost thou?   65
[*Embraces him.*]

ORANGE-WOMAN.

Lord, what a filthy trick these men have got of kissing one
another!   *She spits.*

MEDLEY.

Why do you suffer this cartload of scandal to come near you
and make your neighbors think you so improvident to need
a bawd?   70

ORANGE-WOMAN [*to* Dorimant].

Good, now we shall have it! You did but want him to help

64. with her head] *1704;* with head
Q 1–3.
64. like] *Q 1–3; 1704 omits.*
71. Good . . . You] *Verity;* Good

now, we shall have it, you *Q 1–2;*
Good, now we shall have it; you
Q3; Good, now we shall have it,
you *1704.*

54. *fruz*] wig of short, curled hair.
59. *Change*] the New Exchange, a fashionable arcade of shops off the
Strand.
71. *want*] lack, need.

you. Come, pay me for my fruit.

MEDLEY.

Make us thankful for it, huswife, bawds are as much out of
fashion as gentlemen-ushers: none but old formal ladies use
the one, and none but foppish old stagers employ the other.   75
Go, you are an insignificant brandy bottle.

DORIMANT.

Nay, there you wrong her. Three quarts of canary is her
business.

ORANGE-WOMAN.

What you please, gentlemen.

DORIMANT.

To him! Give him as good as he brings.   80

ORANGE-WOMAN.

Hang him, there is not such another heathen in the town
again, except it be the shoemaker without.

MEDLEY.

I shall see you hold up your hand at the bar next sessions
for murder, huswife. That shoemaker can take his oath you
are in fee with the doctors to sell green fruit to the gentry, 85
that the crudities may breed diseases.

ORANGE-WOMAN.

Pray give me my money.

DORIMANT.

Not a penny! When you bring the gentlewoman hither you
spoke of, you shall be paid.

ORANGE-WOMAN.

The gentlewoman! The gentlewoman may be as honest as   90
your sisters, for aught as I know. Pray pay me, Mr. Dorimant, and do not abuse me so. I have an honester way of
living; you know it.

75. stagers] Q1–3; strangers 1704.   91. sisters] Q1–3; sister 1704.
81. there is] Q1, 1704; there's
Q2–3.

---

73. *Make us thankful*] i.e., God make us thankful.
74. *gentlemen-ushers*] male attendants.
75. *old stagers*] "old hands."
77. *canary*] light, sweet wine from the Canary Islands; with a pun on a
cant meaning of *canary-bird*, a whore.
86. *crudities*] undigested matter in the stomach.
90. *honest*] chaste.

MEDLEY.

Was there ever such a resty bawd?

DORIMANT.

Some jade's tricks she has, but she makes amends when she's   95
in good humor.—Come, tell me the lady's name, and
Handy shall pay you.

ORANGE-WOMAN.

I must not; she forbid me.

DORIMANT.

That's a sure sign she would have you.

MEDLEY.

Where does she live?   100

ORANGE-WOMAN.

They lodge at my house.

MEDLEY.

Nay, then she's in a hopeful way.

ORANGE-WOMAN.

Good Mr. Medley, say your pleasure of me, but take heed
how you affront my house. God's my life, in a hopeful way!

DORIMANT.

Prithee, peace. What kind of woman's the mother?   105

ORANGE-WOMAN.

A goodly, grave gentlewoman. Lord, how she talks against
the wild young men o' the town! As for your part, she thinks
you an arrant devil: should she see you, on my conscience
she would look if you had not a cloven foot.

DORIMANT.

Does she know me?   110

ORANGE-WOMAN.

Only by hearsay. A thousand horrid stories have been told
her of you, and she believes 'em all.

MEDLEY.

By the character, this should be the famous Lady Woodvill
and her daughter Harriet.

ORANGE-WOMAN [aside].

The devil's in him for guessing, I think.   115

107. the town] Q1-2, 1704; th'
town Q3.

94. resty] restive, persistent.

DORIMANT.

Do you know 'em?

MEDLEY.

Both very well. The mother's a great admirer of the forms
and civility of the last age.

DORIMANT.

An antiquated beauty may be allowed to be out of humor
at the freedoms of the present. This is a good account of the   120
mother. Pray, what is the daughter?

MEDLEY.

Why, first, she's an heiress, vastly rich.

DORIMANT.

And handsome?

MEDLEY.

What alteration a twelvemonth may have bred in her, I
know not, but a year ago she was the beautifulest creature I   125
ever saw: a fine, easy, clean shape; light brown hair in
abundance; her features regular; her complexion clear and
lively; large, wanton eyes; but above all, a mouth that
has made me kiss it a thousand times in imagination—
teeth white and even, and pretty, pouting lips, with a   130
little moisture ever hanging on them, that look like the
Provins rose fresh on the bush, ere the morning sun has quite
drawn up the dew.

DORIMANT.

Rapture, mere rapture!

ORANGE-WOMAN.

Nay, gad, he tells you true. She's a delicate creature.   135

DORIMANT.

Has she wit?

MEDLEY.

More than is usual in her sex, and as much malice. Then,
she's as wild as you would wish her, and has a demureness
in her looks that makes it so surprising.

118. civility] *Q1, 1704;* civilities   138. you would] *Q1, 1704;* you'd
Q2–3.   *Q2–3.*

126. *easy*] graceful.   128. *wanton*] lively, roguish.
132. *Provins*] town near Paris, known for its trade in roses.
134. *mere*] absolute, sheer.

DORIMANT.

Flesh and blood cannot hear this and not long to know her. 140

MEDLEY.

I wonder what makes her mother bring her up to town? An
old, doting keeper cannot be more jealous of his mistress.

ORANGE-WOMAN.

She made me laugh yesterday. There was a judge came to
visit 'em, and the old man (she told me) did so stare upon
her and, when he saluted her, smacked so heartily—who 145
would think it of 'em?

MEDLEY.

God-a-mercy, Judge!

DORIMANT.

Do 'em right, the gentlemen of the long robe have not been
wanting by their good examples to countenance the crying
sin o' the nation. 150

MEDLEY.

Come, on with your trappings; 'tis later than you imagine.

DORIMANT.

Call in the shoemaker, Handy!

ORANGE-WOMAN.

Good Mr. Dorimant, pay me. Gad, I had rather give you
my fruit than stay to be abused by that foul-mouthed rogue.
What you gentlemen say, it matters not much; but such a 155
dirty fellow does one more disgrace.

DORIMANT [*to* Handy].

Give her ten shillings. [*To* Orange-Woman.] And be
sure you tell the young gentlewoman I must be acquainted
with her.

ORANGE-WOMAN.

Now do you long to be tempting this pretty creature. Well, 160
heavens mend you!

MEDLEY.

Farewell, bog! *Exeunt* Orange-Woman *and* Handy.

147. God-a-mercy, Judge] *Q 1–3,
1704;* God a mercy, a judge *Verity.*

---

147. *God-a-mercy, Judge*] exclamation of ironic thanks or applause.
148. *gentlemen . . . robe*] lawyers.
162. *bog*] puffy swelling; hence, a fat person.

Dorimant, when did you see your *pis aller*, as you call her,
Mrs. Loveit?

DORIMANT.

Not these two days.   165

MEDLEY.

And how stand affairs between you?

DORIMANT.

There has been great patching of late, much ado; we make a
shift to hang together.

MEDLEY.

I wonder how her mighty spirit bears it?

DORIMANT.

Ill enough, on all conscience. I never knew so violent a   170
creature.

MEDLEY.

She's the most passionate in her love and the most extravagant in her jealousy of any woman I ever heard of. What
note is that?

DORIMANT.

An excuse I am going to send her for the neglect I am guilty   175
of.

MEDLEY.

Prithee, read it.

DORIMANT.

No, but if you will take the pains, you may.

MEDLEY (*reads*).

"I never was a lover of business, but now I have a just reason
to hate it, since it has kept me these two days from seeing   180
you. I intend to wait upon you in the afternoon, and in the
pleasure of your conversation forget all I have suffered
during this tedious absence."—This business of yours,
Dorimant, has been with a vizard at the playhouse; I have
had an eye on you. If some malicious body should betray   185
you, this kind note would hardly make your peace with her.

167. late . . . we] *Verity, Brett-Smith;*   178. you will] *Q 1, 1704;* you'll
late, much ado we *Q 1–2, 1704;* late;   *Q 2–3.*
with much ado we *Q 3.*

---

163. *pis aller*] last resource.
184. *vizard*] mask; often referring to a whore, especially one at the
playhouse.

DORIMANT.

I desire no better.

MEDLEY.

Why, would her knowledge of it oblige you?

DORIMANT.

Most infinitely; next to the coming to a good understanding with a new mistress, I love a quarrel with an old one.   190
But the devil's in't, there has been such a calm in my affairs
of late, I have not had the pleasure of making a woman so
much as break her fan, to be sullen, or forswear herself,
these three days.

MEDLEY.

A very great misfortune! Let me see, I love mischief well   195
enough to forward this business myself. I'll about it presently,
and though I know the truth of what y'ave done will set her
a-raving, I'll heighten it a little with invention, leave her in
a fit o' the mother, and be here again before y'are ready.

DORIMANT.

Pray, stay; you may spare yourself the labor. The business   200
is undertaken already by one who will manage it with as
much address and, I think, with a little more malice than
you can.

MEDLEY.

Who i' the devil's name can this be?

DORIMANT.

Why, the vizard, that very vizard you saw me with.   205

MEDLEY.

Does she love mischief so well as to betray herself to spite
another?

DORIMANT.

Not so neither, Medley; I will make you comprehend the
mystery. This mask, for a farther confirmation of what I
have been these two days swearing to her, made me yester-   210
day at the playhouse make her a promise, before her face,
utterly to break off with Loveit; and because she tenders my
reputation and would not have me do a barbarous thing,
has contrived a way to give me a handome occasion.

---

199. *the mother*] hysteria.
212. *tenders*] cares for.

MEDLEY.

Very good.   215

DORIMANT.

She intends, about an hour before me this afternoon, to make
Loveit a visit; and (having the privilege by reason of a
professed friendship between 'em to talk of her concerns)—

MEDLEY.

Is she a friend?

DORIMANT.

Oh, an intimate friend!   220

MEDLEY.

Better and better! Pray proceed.

DORIMANT.

She means insensibly to insinuate a discourse of me and
artificially raise her jealousy to such a height that, transported with the first motions of her passion, she shall fly
upon me with all the fury imaginable as soon as ever I enter. 225
The quarrel being thus happily begun, I am to play my
part: confess and justify all my roguery, swear her impertinence and ill humor makes her intolerable, tax her with
the next fop that comes into my head, and in a huff march
away, slight her, and leave her to be taken by whosoever 230
thinks it worth his time to lie down before her.

MEDLEY.

This vizard is a spark, and has a genius that makes her
worthy of yourself, Dorimant.

        Enter Handy, Shoemaker, *and Footman.*

DORIMANT [*to Footman*].

You rogue there, who sneak like a dog that has flung down
a dish! If you do not mend your waiting, I'll uncase you 235
and turn you loose to the wheel of fortune.—Handy, seal
this and let him run with it presently.   *Exit Footman.*

MEDLEY.

Since y'are resolved on a quarrel, why do you send her this
kind note?

218. 'em to ... concerns)] *Q1–2,*   concerns *Q3, 1704, Verity.*
Brett-Smith; 'em) to talk of her

───────────────────────────────

223. *artificially*] artfully.   232. *genius*] spirit, character.
235. *uncase you*] strip you (of livery).

DORIMANT.

To keep her at home in order to the business. (*To the* 240
Shoemaker.) How now, you drunken sot?

SHOEMAKER.

'Zbud, you have no reason to talk. I have not had a bottle
of sack of yours in my belly this fortnight.

MEDLEY.

The orange-woman says your neighbors take notice what
a heathen you are, and design to inform the bishop and have 245
you burned for an atheist.

SHOEMAKER.

Damn her, dunghill! If her husband does not remove her,
she stinks so, the parish intend to indict him for a nuisance.

MEDLEY.

I advise you like a friend, reform your life. You have brought
the envy of the world upon you by living above yourself. 250
Whoring and swearing are vices too genteel for a shoemaker.

SHOEMAKER.

'Zbud, I think you men of quality will grow as unreasonable
as the women: you would engross the sins o' the nation.
Poor folks can no sooner be wicked but th'are railed at by 255
their betters.

DORIMANT.

Sirrah, I'll have you stand i' the pillory for this libel.

SHOEMAKER.

Some of you deserve it, I'm sure. There are so many of 'em
that our journeymen nowadays, instead of harmless ballads,
sing nothing but your damned lampoons. 260

DORIMANT.

Our lampoons, you rogue?

SHOEMAKER.

Nay, good master, why should not you write your own
commentaries as well as Caesar?

255. th'are] *Q1–2;* they're *Q3,*
1704.

---

242. *'Zbud*] 'Sblood; contraction of "God's blood."
254. *engross*] monopolize.
263. *commentaries*] with a pun on two meanings of "commentary":
1) expository treatise; 2) illustrative or satiric "comment."

MEDLEY.

The rascal's read, I perceive.

SHOEMAKER.

You know the old proverb, ale and history.   265

DORIMANT.

Draw on my shoes, sirrah.

SHOEMAKER.

Here's a shoe—

DORIMANT.

Sits with more wrinkles than there are in an angry bully's
forehead.

SHOEMAKER.

'Zbud, as smooth as your mistress's skin does upon her. So,   270
strike your foot in home. 'Zbud, if e'er a monsieur of 'em all
make more fashionable ware, I'll be content to have my
ears whipped off with my own paring knife.

MEDLEY.

And served up in a ragout, instead of coxcombs, to a company of French shoemakers for a collation.   275

SHOEMAKER.

Hold, hold! Damn 'em caterpillars, let 'em feed upon
cabbage!—Come master, your health this morning next my
heart now.

DORIMANT.

Go, get you home, and govern your family better! Do not
let your wife follow you to the alehouse, beat your whore,   280
and lead you home in triumph.

SHOEMAKER.

'Zbud, there's never a man i' the town lives more like a

272. to have] *Q1-2, 1704;* t'ave   now! *Brett-Smith.*
Q3.   281. you] *Q1-2, 1704;* her *Q3.*
277-278. morning . . . now.] *Q1-3,* 282. the] *Q1, 1704;* th' *Q2-3.*
1704; morning! next my heart,

---

265. *the old . . . history*] "Truth is in ale as in history" (Tilley, p. 686).
G. L. Apperson, *English Proverbs and Proverbial Phrases* [London, 1929], p. 4,
cites the same references as Tilley but regards them as insufficient evidence
to identify the proverb.

276. *caterpillars*] covetous persons, parasites.

277-278. *your . . . now*] The shoemaker asks Dorimant for money to drink
his health; *next my heart* may refer to a toast drunk with hand on heart.

gentleman with his wife than I do. I never mind her motions;
she never inquires into mine. We speak to one another civilly,
hate one another heartily, and because 'tis vulgar to lie and   285
soak together, we have each of us our several settle-bed.

DORIMANT [*to* Handy].

Give him half a crown.

MEDLEY.

Not without he will promise to be bloody drunk.

SHOEMAKER.

Tope's the word, i' the eye of the world.   [*To* Handy.]
For my master's honor, Robin!   290

DORIMANT.

Do not debauch my servants, sirrah.

SHOEMAKER.

I only tip him the wink; he knows an alehouse from a hovel.

Exit Shoemaker.

DORIMANT [*to* Handy].

My clothes, quickly!

MEDLEY.

Where shall we dine today?

Enter Young Bellair.

DORIMANT.

Where you will. Here comes a good third man.   295

YOUNG BELLAIR.

Your servant, gentlemen.

284. to one another] *Q1, 1704;*
one to another *Q2;* to another *Q3.*
288. he will] *Q1–2, 1704;* he'll *Q3.*
289–290. Tope's . . . Robin] Tope's
the word i' the eye of the world for

my master's honor Robin *Q1;*
Q2–3 add a comma after honor; *1704*
adds commas after world *and* honor.
291. servants] *Q1–2, 1704;* servant
Q3.

283. *motions*] activities.   286. *soak*] drink.
286. *settle-bed*] wooden bench, convertible to a bed.
288. *without*] unless.
289–290. *Tope's . . . Robin*] See textual note. Brett-Smith thinks the shoemaker reproves Medley for saying *bloody drunk*; i.e., "tope" is the word a
gentleman should use (for the sake of his "honor"?). The text as printed
here follows Brett-Smith's suggestion that the shoemaker may pause after
world, then with a wink invite Handy to join him. Possibly "tope" is used
in its sense as an exclamation, equivalent to "I pledge you." In that case,
the shoemaker accepts Medley's conditions, as (he asserts) would *the world.*
Cf. *tope* (Fr.), to indicate acceptance of a wager or a pledge in drinking.

MEDLEY.

Gentle sir, how will you answer this visit to your honorable
mistress? 'Tis not her interest you should keep company
with men of sense, who will be talking reason.

YOUNG BELLAIR.

I do not fear her pardon, do you but grant me yours for my   300
neglect of late.

MEDLEY.

Though y'ave made us miserable by the want of your good
company, to show you I am free from all resentment, may
the beautiful cause of our misfortune give you all the joys
happy lovers have shared ever since the world began.   305

YOUNG BELLAIR.

You wish me in heaven, but you believe me on my journey
to hell.

MEDLEY.

You have a good strong faith, and that may contribute
much towards your salvation. I confess I am but of an
untoward constitution, apt to have doubts and scruples;   310
and in love they are no less distracting than in religion.
Were I so near marriage, I should cry out by fits as I ride
in my coach, "Cuckold, cuckold!" with no less fury than
the mad fanatic does "Glory!" in Bethlem.

YOUNG BELLAIR.

Because religion makes some run mad, must I live an   315
atheist?

MEDLEY.

Is it not great indiscretion for a man of credit, who may
have money enough on his word, to go and deal with Jews,
who for little sums make men enter into bonds and give
judgments?   320

309. towards] *Q1, 1704;* toward   *Q2-3.*
Q2-3.   315. live an] *Q1-2, 1704;* live like
310. untoward] *Q1, 1704;* outward   an *Q3.*

310. *untoward constitution*] i.e., not inclined to religion.
314. *mad . . . Bethlem*] Brett-Smith identifies the *fanatic* as Oliver
Cromwell's mad porter; cf. Matthew Prior's "Dialogue between Oliver
Cromwell and his Porter." Bethlem is Bethlehem Hospital, the insane
asylum known usually as Bedlam.
319-320. *give judgments*] assign chattels as security.

YOUNG BELLAIR.

Preach no more on this text; I am determined, and there is no hope of my conversion.

DORIMANT (*to* Handy, *who is fiddling about him*).

Leave your unnecessary fiddling. A wasp that's buzzing about a man's nose at dinner is not more troublesome than thou art.   325

HANDY.

You love to have your clothes hang just, sir.

DORIMANT.

I love to be well-dressed, sir, and think it no scandal to my understanding.

HANDY.

Will you use the essence, or orange-flower water?

DORIMANT.

I will smell as I do today, no offense to the ladies' noses.   330

HANDY.

Your pleasure, sir.   [*Exit* Handy.]

DORIMANT.

That a man's excellency should lie in neatly tying of a ribbon or a cravat! How careful's nature in furnishing the world with necessary coxcombs!

YOUNG BELLAIR.

That's a mighty pretty suit of yours, Dorimant.   335

DORIMANT.

I am glad 't has your approbation.

YOUNG BELLAIR.

No man in town has a better fancy in his clothes than you have.

DORIMANT.

You will make me have an opinion of my genius.

MEDLEY.

There is a great critic, I hear, in these matters lately arrived   340 piping hot from Paris.

YOUNG BELLAIR.

Sir Fopling Flutter, you mean.

---

329. *essence*] perfume.
334. *necessary coxcombs*] natural coxcombs, who cannot be other than they are.

MEDLEY.

The same.

YOUNG BELLAIR.

He thinks himself the pattern of modern gallantry.

DORIMANT.

He is indeed the pattern of modern foppery.   345

MEDLEY.

He was yesterday at the play, with a pair of gloves up to his elbows and a periwig more exactly curled than a lady's head newly dressed for a ball.

YOUNG BELLAIR.

What a pretty lisp he has!

DORIMANT.

Ho, that he affects in imitation of the people of quality of 350 France.

MEDLEY.

His head stands for the most part on one side, and his looks are more languishing than a lady's when she lolls at stretch in her coach or leans her head carelessly against the side of a box i' the playhouse.   355

DORIMANT.

He is a person indeed of great acquired follies.

MEDLEY.

He is like many others, beholding to his education for making him so eminent a coxcomb. Many a fool had been lost to the world, had their indulgent parents wisely bestowed neither learning nor good breeding on 'em.   360

YOUNG BELLAIR.

He has been, as the sparkish word is, brisk upon the ladies already. He was yesterday at my Aunt Townley's and gave Mrs. Loveit a catalogue of his good qualities, under the character of a complete gentleman, who (according to Sir Fopling) ought to dress well, dance well, fence well, have a 365 genius for love letters, an agreeable voice for a chamber, be very amorous, something discreet, but not overconstant.

MEDLEY.

Pretty ingredients to make an accomplished person!

350–351. of France] *Q1–3;* in   357. beholding] *Q1–2, 1704;* be-
France *1704.*   holden *Q3.*

DORIMANT.

I am glad he pitched upon Loveit.

YOUNG BELLAIR.

How so? 370

DORIMANT.

I wanted a fop to lay to her charge; and this is as pat as may be.

YOUNG BELLAIR.

I am confident she loves no man but you.

DORIMANT.

The good fortune were enough to make me vain, but that I am in my nature modest. 375

YOUNG BELLAIR.

Hark you, Dorimant.—With your leave, Mr. Medley. 'Tis only a secret concerning a fair lady.

MEDLEY.

Your good breeding, sir, gives you too much trouble. You might have whispered without all this ceremony.

YOUNG BELLAIR (to Dorimant).

How stand your affairs with Bellinda of late? 380

DORIMANT.

She's a little jilting baggage.

YOUNG BELLAIR.

Nay, I believe her false enough, but she's ne'er the worse for your purpose. She was with you yesterday in a disguise at the play.

DORIMANT.

There we fell out and resolved never to speak to one 385 another more.

YOUNG BELLAIR.

The occasion?

DORIMANT.

Want of courage to meet me at the place appointed. These young women apprehend loving as much as the young men do fighting at first; but once entered, like them too, they all 390 turn bullies straight.

Enter Handy.

─────────────────────────────

369. *pitched upon*] "set his sights on."

HANDY (*to* Young Bellair).

Sir, your man without desires to speak with you.

YOUNG BELLAIR.

Gentlemen, I'll return immediately.   *Exit* Young Bellair.

MEDLEY.

A very pretty fellow, this.

DORIMANT.

He's handsome, well-bred, and by much the most tolerable 395
of all the young men that do not abound in wit.

MEDLEY.

Ever well-dressed, always complaisant, and seldom imper-
tinent; you and he are grown very intimate, I see.

DORIMANT.

It is our mutual interest to be so. It makes the women think
the better of his understanding and judge more favorably of 400
my reputation; it makes him pass upon some for a man of
very good sense, and I upon others for a very civil person.

MEDLEY.

What was that whisper?

DORIMANT.

A thing which he would fain have known, but I did not
think it fit to tell him. It might have frighted him from his 405
honorable intentions of marrying.

MEDLEY.

Emilia, give her her due, has the best reputation of any
young woman about the town who has beauty enough to
provoke detraction. Her carriage is unaffected, her discourse
modest—not at all censorious nor pretending, like the 410
counterfeits of the age.

DORIMANT.

She's a discreet maid, and I believe nothing can corrupt her
but a husband.

MEDLEY.

A husband?

DORIMANT.

Yes, a husband. I have known many women make a dif- 415
ficulty of losing a maidenhead, who have afterwards made
none of making a cuckold.

404. which] *Q 1, 1704;* that *Q 2–3.*   417. making] *Q 1–3; 1704 omits.*

409. *carriage*] behavior.

MEDLEY.

This prudent consideration, I am apt to think, has made
you confirm poor Bellair in the desperate resolution he has
taken.   420

DORIMANT.

Indeed, the little hope I found there was of her, in the state
she was in, has made me by my advice contribute something
towards the changing of her condition.

Enter Young Bellair.

Dear Bellair, by heavens I thought we had lost thee! Men
in love are never to be reckoned on when we would form a 425
company.

YOUNG BELLAIR.

Dorimant, I am undone. My man has brought the most
surprising news i' the world.

DORIMANT.

Some strange misfortune is befall'n your love?

YOUNG BELLAIR.

My father came to town last night and lodges i' the very 430
house where Emilia lies.

MEDLEY.

Does he know it is with her you are in love?

YOUNG BELLAIR.

He knows I love, but knows not whom, without some
officious sot has betrayed me.

DORIMANT.

Your Aunt Townley is your confidante and favors the 435
business.

YOUNG BELLAIR.

I do not apprehend any ill office from her. I have received
a letter, in which I am commanded by my father to meet
him at my aunt's this afternoon. He tells me farther he has
made a match for me, and bids me resolve to be obedient 440
to his will or expect to be disinherited.

MEDLEY.

Now's your time, Bellair. Never had lover such an oppor-

422. me] *Q 1–3;* him *1704.*

tunity of giving a generous proof of his passion.

YOUNG BELLAIR.

As how, I pray?

MEDLEY.

Why, hang an estate, marry Emilia out of hand, and pro- 445
voke your father to do what he threatens. 'Tis but despising
a coach, humbling yourself to a pair of galoshes, being out
of countenance when you meet your friends, pointed at and
pitied wherever you go by all the amorous fops that know
you, and your fame will be immortal.   450

YOUNG BELLAIR.

I could find in my heart to resolve not to marry at all.

DORIMANT.

Fie, fie! That would spoil a good jest and disappoint the
well-natured town of an occasion of laughing at you.

YOUNG BELLAIR.

The storm I have so long expected hangs o'er my head and
begins to pour down upon me. I am on the rack and can 455
have no rest till I'm satisfied in what I fear. Where do you
dine?

DORIMANT.

At Long's or Locket's.

MEDLEY.

At Long's let it be.

YOUNG BELLAIR.

I'll run and see Emilia and inform myself how matters 460
stand. If my misfortunes are not so great as to make me unfit
for company, I'll be with you.   *Exit* Young Bellair.

Enter a Footman, *with a letter.*

FOOTMAN [*to* Dorimant].

Here's a letter, sir.

DORIMANT.

The superscription's right: "For Mr. Dorimant."

MEDLEY.

Let's see. [*Looks at the letter.*]   The very scrawl and spell- 465
ing of a true-bred whore.

---

447. *galoshes*] rustic shoes or overshoes, usually with wooden soles.
458. *Long's or Locket's*] fashionable taverns.

DORIMANT.

I know the hand. The style is admirable, I assure you.

MEDLEY.

Prithee, read it.

DORIMANT (*reads*).

"I told a you you dud not love me, if you dud, you would
have seen me again ere now. I have no money and am very 470
malicolly. Pray send me a guynie to see the operies. Your
servant to command, Molly."

MEDLEY.

Pray let the whore have a favorable answer, that she may
spark it in a box and do honor to her profession.

DORIMANT.

She shall, and perk up i' the face of quality. [*To* Handy.] 475
Is the coach at door?

HANDY.

You did not bid me send for it.

DORIMANT.

Eternal blockhead!

Handy *offers to go out.*

Hey, sot!

HANDY.

Did you call me, sir?   480

DORIMANT.

I hope you have no just exception to the name, sir?

HANDY.

I have sense, sir.

DORIMANT.

Not so much as a fly in winter.—How did you come,
Medley?

MEDLEY.

In a chair.   485

FOOTMAN.

You may have a hackney coach if you please, sir.

DORIMANT.

I may ride the elephant if I please, sir. Call another chair

---

475. *perk up*] behave impudently or boldly; strut.

487. *I . . . elephant*] perhaps a topical reference; elephants were sometimes
exhibited as a popular curiosity.

and let my coach follow to Long's.
                    [*Exeunt* Footman *and* Handy.]
          "Be calm, ye great parents, etc."
                              Exeunt, singing.

---

489. *Be . . . etc.*] I have been unable to trace this song.

Act II

[*Lady Townley's house.*] *Enter my* Lady Townley *and* Emilia.

LADY TOWNLEY.

I was afraid, Emilia, all had been discovered.

EMILIA.

I tremble with the apprehension still.

LADY TOWNLEY.

That my brother should take lodgings i' the very house where you lie!

EMILIA.

'Twas lucky we had timely notice to warn the people to be   5
secret. He seems to be a mighty good-humored old man.

LADY TOWNLEY.

He ever had a notable smirking way with him.

EMILIA.

He calls me rogue, tells me he can't abide me, and does so bepat me.

LADY TOWNLEY.

On my word, you are much in his favor then.   10

EMILIA.

He has been very inquisitive, I am told, about my family, my reputation, and my fortune.

LADY TOWNLEY.

I am confident he does not i' the least suspect you are the woman his son's in love with.

EMILIA.

What should make him then inform himself so particularly   15
of me?

LADY TOWNLEY.

He was always of a very loving temper himself. It may be he has a doting fit upon him, who knows?

EMILIA.

It cannot be.

Enter Young Bellair.

LADY TOWNLEY.

Here comes my nephew.——Where did you leave your   20
father?

YOUNG BELLAIR.

Writing a note within.—Emilia, this early visit looks as if some kind jealousy would not let you rest at home.

EMILIA.

The knowledge I have of my rival gives me a little cause to fear your constancy.   25

YOUNG BELLAIR.

My constancy! I vow—

EMILIA.

Do not vow. Our love is frail as is our life, and full as little in our power; and are you sure you shall outlive this day?

YOUNG BELLAIR.

I am not, but when we are in perfect health, 'twere an idle thing to fright ourselves with the thoughts of sudden death.   30

LADY TOWNLEY.

Pray, what has passed between you and your father i' the garden?

YOUNG BELLAIR.

He's firm in his resolution, tells me I must marry Mrs. Harriet, or swears he'll marry himself and disinherit me. When I saw I could not prevail with him to be more indul-   35 gent, I dissembled an obedience to his will, which has composed his passion and will give us time—and I hope opportunity—to deceive him.

Enter Old Bellair, *with a note in his hand.*

LADY TOWNLEY.

Peace, here he comes.

OLD BELLAIR.

Harry, take this and let your man carry it for me to Mr.   40 Fourbe's chamber—my lawyer, i' the Temple.

[*Exit* Young Bellair.]

(*To* Emilia.)   Neighbor, adod I am glad to see thee here. —Make much of her, sister. She's one of the best of your acquaintance. I like her countenance and behavior well;

40–41. *Mr. Fourbe's*] The name is from *fourb(e)*, a cheat.

41. *the Temple*] originally, the property of the Knights Templars; since the fourteenth century, center for the legal profession in London.

42. *adod*] The interjection is equivalent to "egad."

she has a modesty that is not common i' this age, adod she   45
has.

LADY TOWNLEY.

I know her value, brother, and esteem her accordingly.

OLD BELLAIR.

Advise her to wear a little more mirth in her face. Adod,
she's too serious.

LADY TOWNLEY.

The fault is very excusable in a young woman.   50

OLD BELLAIR.

Nay, adod, I like her ne'er the worse; a melancholy beauty
has her charms. I love a pretty sadness in a face which
varies now and then, like changeable colors, into a smile.

LADY TOWNLEY.

Methinks you speak very feelingly, brother.

OLD BELLAIR.

I am but five-and-fifty, sister, you know—an age not   55
altogether insensible. (*To* Emilia.)   Cheer up, sweetheart,
I have a secret to tell thee may chance to make thee merry.
We three will make collation together anon. I' the meantime, mum! [*Aloud.*]   I can't abide you; go, I can't abide
you.   60

Enter Young Bellair.

Harry! Come, you must along with me to my Lady Woodvill's.—I am going to slip the boy at a mistress.

YOUNG BELLAIR.

At a wife, sir, you would say.

OLD BELLAIR.

You need not look so glum, sir. A wife is no curse when she
brings the blessing of a good estate with her. But an idle   65
town flirt, with a painted face, a rotten reputation, and a

58–59. I' ... you] I' the meantime   mum; I can't abide you *CBEP, O.*
mum, I can't abide you *Q1–2, 1704;*   61. my] *Q1, 1704; Q2–3 omit.*
In the meantime, mum, I can't   64. glum] *Q1–3;* grum *1704.*
abide you *Q3;* I' the meantime

59. *mum*] See textual note. Two readings of *mum* are possible: 1) an
injunction to silence (the reading assumed in this text); 2) a colloquial
variant of "ma'am."
62. *slip*] release, as from a leash.

crazy fortune, adod, is the devil and all; and such a one I
hear you are in league with.

YOUNG BELLAIR.

I cannot help detraction, sir.

OLD BELLAIR.

Out, a pize o' their breeches, there are keeping fools   70
enough for such flaunting baggages, and they are e'en too
good for 'em. (*To* Emilia.) Remember night. [*Aloud.*]
Go, y'are a rogue, y'are a rogue. Fare you well, fare you
well. [*To* Young Bellair.] Come, come, come along, sir.
                         Exeunt Old *and* Young Bellair.

LADY TOWNLEY.

On my word, the old man comes on apace. I'll lay my life   75
he's smitten.

EMILIA.

This is nothing but the pleasantness of his humor.

LADY TOWNLEY.

I know him better than you. Let it work; it may prove
lucky.
                         Enter a Page.

PAGE.

Madam, Mr. Medley has sent to know whether a visit will   80
not be troublesome this afternoon?

LADY TOWNLEY.

Send him word his visits never are so.   [*Exit* Page.]

EMILIA.

He's a very pleasant man.

LADY TOWNLEY.

He's a very necessary man among us women. He's not
scandalous i' the least, perpetually contriving to bring good 85
company together, and always ready to stop up a gap at
ombre. Then, he knows all the little news o' the town.

EMILIA.

I love to hear him talk o' the intrigues. Let 'em be never so

73–74. Fare you well, fare you   87. o'] *Q1, 1704;* i' *Q2–3.*
well] *Q1, 1704;* Fare you well   88. 'em] *Q1–2, 1704;* them *Q3.*
Q2–3.

---

70. *a pize*] imprecation of uncertain meaning; cf. "a pox."
70. *keeping fools*] fools who keep mistresses.
87. *ombre*] card game for three players.

dull in themselves, he'll make 'em pleasant i' the relation.

LADY TOWNLEY.

But he improves things so much one can take no measure of 90
the truth from him. Mr. Dorimant swears a flea or a maggot
is not made more monstrous by a magnifying glass than a
story is by his telling it.

Enter Medley.

EMILIA.

Hold, here he comes.

LADY TOWNLEY.

Mr. Medley. 95

MEDLEY.

Your servant, madam.

LADY TOWNLEY.

You have made yourself a stranger of late.

EMILIA.

I believe you took a surfeit of ombre last time you were here.

MEDLEY.

Indeed I had my bellyful of that termagant, Lady Dealer.
There never was so insatiable a carder; an old gleeker never 100
loved to sit to 't like her. I have played with her, now at
least a dozen times, till she 'as worn out all her fine complexion and her tour would keep in curl no longer.

LADY TOWNLEY.

Blame her not, poor woman. She loves nothing so well as a
black ace. 105

MEDLEY.

The pleasure I have seen her in when she has had hope in
drawing for a matadore!

EMILIA.

'Tis as pretty sport to her as persuading masks off is to you,
to make discoveries.

98. of] *Q1, 1704;* at *Q2–3.*   108. as pretty] *Q1–2, 1704;* a
pretty *Q3.*

---

100. *carder*] card player.
100. *gleeker*] Gleek is a card game.
103. *tour*] crescent-shaped front of false hair.
107. *matadore*] In ombre, the highest trumps (the black aces and a
variable third card) were called matadores.

LADY TOWNLEY.

Pray, where's your friend Mr. Dorimant?   110

MEDLEY.

Soliciting his affairs. He's a man of great employment—has more mistresses now depending than the most eminent lawyer in England has causes.

EMILIA.

Here has been Mrs. Loveit so uneasy and out of humor these two days.   115

LADY TOWNLEY.

How strangely love and jealousy rage in that poor woman!

MEDLEY.

She could not have picked out a devil upon earth so proper to torment her. H'as made her break a dozen or two of fans already, tear half a score points in pieces, and destroy hoods and knots without number.   120

LADY TOWNLEY.

We heard of a pleasant serenade he gave her t'other night.

MEDLEY.

A Danish serenade, with kettledrums and trumpets.

EMILIA.

Oh, barbarous!

MEDLEY.

What, you are of the number of the ladies whose ears are grown so delicate since our operas, you can be charmed 125 with nothing but *flûtes douces* and French hautboys?

EMILIA.

Leave your raillery and tell us, is there any new wit come forth—songs, or novels?

MEDLEY.

A very pretty piece of gallantry, by an eminent author, called

118. H'as] *Q3;* has *Q1–2;* He has
1704.

---

112. *depending*] pending, like a lawyer's *causes* (cases).
119. *points*] pieces of lace.   120. *knots*] bows of ribbon.
122. *A Danish . . . trumpets*] See *Hamlet,* I.iv.8–12: "The King doth wake tonight and takes his rouse,/ Keeps wassail, and the swaggering upspring reels;/ And as he drains his draughts of Rhenish down,/ The kettledrum and trumpet thus bray out/ The triumph of his pledge."
126. *flûtes douces*] high-pitched flutes.   126. *hautboys*] oboes.

The Diversions of Brussels—very necessary to be read by all 130
old ladies who are desirous to improve themselves at questions and commands, blindman's buff, and the like fashionable recreations.

EMILIA.

Oh, ridiculous!

MEDLEY.

Then there is *The Art of Affectation*, written by a late beauty 135
of quality, teaching you how to draw up your breasts,
stretch up your neck, to thrust out your breech, to play with
your head, to toss up your nose, to bite your lips, to turn up
your eyes, to speak in a silly soft tone of a voice, and use all
the foolish French words that will infallibly make your 140
person and conversation charming; with a short apology
at the latter end, in the behalf of young ladies who notoriously wash and paint, though they have naturally good
complexions.

EMILIA.

What a deal of stuff you tell us!   145

MEDLEY.

Such as the town affords, madam. The Russians, hearing
the great respect we have for foreign dancing, have lately
sent over some of their best balladines, who are now practicing a famous ballet which will be suddenly danced at the
Bear Garden.   150

LADY TOWNLEY.

Pray forbear your idle stories, and give us an account of the
state of love as it now stands.

MEDLEY.

Truly there has been some revolutions in those affairs: great
chopping and changing among the old, and some new

---

130. *The . . . Brussels*] an invention of Medley's, as is *The Art of Affectation*
(l. 135, below).

131–132. *questions and commands*] game in which one player addressed
ludicrous questions and commands to the others.

143. *wash*] use cosmetic washes.

148. *balladines*] ballet dancers.   149. *suddenly*] soon.

150. *Bear Garden*] an amphitheater for bear-baiting, on Bankside.

154. *chopping and changing*] The phrase meant, originally, "bartering
with, trading"; here it keeps something of that meaning.

lovers, whom malice, indiscretion, and misfortune have 155
luckily brought into play.

LADY TOWNLEY.

What think you of walking into the next room and sitting
down, before you engage in this business?

MEDLEY.

I wait upon you; and I hope (though women are commonly unreasonable) by the plenty of scandal I shall dis- 160
cover, to give you very good content, ladies.   *Exeunt.*

[II.ii]

[*Mrs. Loveit's.*] *Enter* Mrs. Loveit *and* Pert; Mrs. Loveit *putting up
a letter, then pulling out her pocket glass and looking in it.*

MRS. LOVEIT.

Pert.

PERT.

Madam?

MRS. LOVEIT.

I hate myself, I look so ill today.

PERT.

Hate the wicked cause on't, that base man Mr. Dorimant,
who makes you torment and vex yourself continually.   5

MRS. LOVEIT.

He is to blame, indeed.

PERT.

To blame to be two days without sending, writing, or
coming near you, contrary to his oath and covenant! 'Twas
to much purpose to make him swear! I'll lay my life there's
not an article but he has broken: talked to the vizards i' the 10
pit, waited upon the ladies from the boxes to their coaches,
gone behind the scenes and fawned upon those little insignificant creatures, the players. 'Tis impossible for a man of
his inconstant temper to forbear, I'm sure.

MRS. LOVEIT.

I know he is a devil, but he has something of the angel yet 15
undefaced in him, which makes him so charming and

15. he is] *Q1, 1704;* he's *Q2–3.*

0.1. *putting up*] putting away.

agreeable that I must love him, be he never so wicked.

PERT.

I little thought, madam, to see your spirit tamed to this degree, who banished poor Mr. Lackwit but for taking up another lady's fan in your presence. 20

MRS. LOVEIT.

My knowing of such odious fools contributes to the making of me love Dorimant the better.

PERT.

Your knowing of Mr. Dorimant, in my mind, should rather make you hate all mankind.

MRS. LOVEIT.

So it does, besides himself. 25

PERT.

Pray, what excuse does he make in his letter?

MRS. LOVEIT.

He has had business.

PERT.

Business in general terms would not have been a current excuse for another. A modish man is always very busy when he is in pursuit of a new mistress. 30

MRS. LOVEIT.

Some fop has bribed you to rail at him. He had business; I will believe it and will forgive him.

PERT.

You may forgive him anything, but I shall never forgive him his turning me into ridicule, as I hear he does.

MRS. LOVEIT.

I perceive you are of the number of those fools his wit has 35 made his enemies.

PERT.

I am of the number of those he's pleased to rally, madam; and if we may believe Mr. Wagfan and Mr. Caperwell, he sometimes makes merry with yourself, too, among his laughing companions. 40

MRS. LOVEIT.

Blockheads are as malicious to witty men as ugly women are

30. he is] *Q1, 1704;* he's *Q2-3.*   35. has] *1704;* had *Q1-3.*

28. *current*] acceptable.

to the handsome; 'tis their interest, and they make it their
business to defame 'em.

PERT.

I wish Mr. Dorimant would not make it his business to
defame you.   45

MRS. LOVEIT.

Should he, I had rather be made infamous by him than owe
my reputation to the dull discretion of those fops you talk
of.

                          Enter Bellinda.

Bellinda!

                                              Running to her.

BELLINDA.

My dear!   50

MRS. LOVEIT.

You have been unkind of late.

BELLINDA.

Do not say unkind, say unhappy.

MRS. LOVEIT.

I could chide you. Where have you been these two days?

BELLINDA.

Pity me rather, my dear, where I have been so tired with
two or three country gentlewomen, whose conversation has   55
been more insufferable than a country fiddle.

MRS. LOVEIT.

Are they relations?

BELLINDA.

No, Welsh acquaintance I made when I was last year at St.
Winifred's. They have asked me a thousand questions of the
modes and intrigues of the town, and I have told 'em almost   60
as many things for news that hardly were so when their
gowns were in fashion.

MRS. LOVEIT.

Provoking creatures, how could you endure 'em?

48. of] *Q3;* off *Q1–2, 1704.*

58–59. *St. Winifred's*] The Welsh town of Holywell takes its name from
St. Winifred's well, believed to have risen where the head of St. Winifred
fell, cut off by a pagan prince she had rejected.

BELLINDA (*aside*).

Now to carry on my plot; nothing but love could make me
capable of so much falsehood. 'Tis time to begin, lest   65
Dorimant should come before her jealousy has stung her.

Laughs and then speaks on.

I was yesterday at a play with 'em, where I was fain to
show 'em the living, as the man at Westminster does the
dead. That is Mrs. Such-a-one, admired for her beauty;
this is Mr. Such-a-one, cried up for a wit; that is sparkish   70
Mr. Such-a-one, who keeps reverend Mrs. Such-a-one; and
there sits fine Mrs. Such-a-one, who was lately cast off by
my Lord Such-a-one.

MRS. LOVEIT.

Did you see Dorimant there?

BELLINDA.

I did; and imagine you were there with him and have no   75
mind to own it.

MRS. LOVEIT.

What should make you think so?

BELLINDA.

A lady masked, in a pretty *déshabillé*, whom Dorimant
entertained with more respect than the gallants do a common vizard.   80

MRS. LOVEIT (*aside*).

Dorimant at the play entertaining a mask! Oh, heavens!

BELLINDA (*aside*).

Good!

MRS. LOVEIT.

Did he stay all the while?

BELLINDA.

Till the play was done, and then led her out; which confirms
me it was you.   85

MRS. LOVEIT.

Traitor!

PERT.

Now you may believe he had business, and you may forgive
him too.

---

68. *man at Westminster*] guide at Westminster Abbey.
78. *in . . . déshabillé*] in a "revealing" dress.

MRS. LOVEIT.

Ungrateful, perjured man!

BELLINDA.

You seem so much concerned, my dear, I fear I have told   90
you unawares what I had better have concealed for your
quiet.

MRS. LOVEIT.

What manner of shape had she?

BELLINDA.

Tall and slender. Her motions were very genteel. Certainly
she must be some person of condition.   95

MRS. LOVEIT.

Shame and confusion be ever in her face when she shows it!

BELLINDA.

I should blame your discretion for loving that wild man, my
dear; but they say he has a way so bewitching that few can
defend their hearts who know him.

MRS. LOVEIT.

I will tear him from mine, or die i' the attempt!   100

BELLINDA.

Be more moderate.

MRS. LOVEIT.

Would I had daggers, darts, or poisoned arrows in my
breast, so I could but remove the thoughts of him from
thence!

BELLINDA.

Fie, fie, your transports are too violent, my dear. This may 105
be but an accidental gallantry, and 'tis likely ended at her
coach.

PERT.

Should it proceed farther, let your comfort be, the conduct
Mr. Dorimant affects will quickly make you know your rival,
ten to one let you see her ruined, her reputation exposed to 110
the town—a happiness none will envy her but yourself,
madam.

MRS. LOVEIT.

Whoe'er she be, all the harm I wish her is, may she love him
as well as I do, and may he give her as much cause to hate
him!   115

94. were] Q1–3; 1704 omits.

PERT.

Never doubt the latter end of your curse, madam.

MRS. LOVEIT.

May all the passions that are raised by neglected love—
jealousy, indignation, spite, and thirst of revenge—eternally
rage in her soul, as they do now in mine!

Walks up and down with a distracted air.

Enter a Page.

PAGE.

Madam, Mr. Dorimant—   120

MRS. LOVEIT.

I will not see him.

PAGE.

I told him you were within, madam.

MRS. LOVEIT.

Say you lied, say I'm busy—shut the door—say anything!

PAGE.

He's here, madam.

Enter Dorimant.   [*Exit* Page.]

DORIMANT.

"They taste of death who do at heaven arrive;   125
But we this paradise approach alive."

(*To* Mrs. Loveit.)   What, dancing the galloping nag without a fiddle?

Offers to catch her by the hand; she flings away and walks on.

I fear this restlessness of the body, madam, (*pursuing her*)
proceeds from an unquietness of the mind. What unlucky 130
accident puts you out of humor—a point ill-washed, knots
spoiled i' the making up, hair shaded awry, or some other
little mistake in setting you in order?

PERT.

A trifle, in my opinion, sir, more inconsiderable than any
you mention.   135

DORIMANT.

Oh, Mrs. Pert! I never knew you sullen enough to be
silent. Come, let me know the business.

125–126. *They . . . alive*] Waller, "Of her Chamber," ll. 1–2 (Thorn
Drury, I, 26). Dorimant substitutes *who* for the original "that."
127. *galloping nag*] country dance.

PERT.

The business, sir, is the business that has taken you up these
two days. How have I seen you laugh at men of business,
and now to become a man of business yourself!   140

DORIMANT.

We are not masters of our own affections; our inclinations
daily alter. Now we love pleasure, and anon we shall dote on
business. Human frailty will have it so, and who can help it?

MRS. LOVEIT.

Faithless, inhuman, barbarous man—

DORIMANT [aside].

Good. Now the alarm strikes.   145

MRS. LOVEIT.

—Without sense of love, of honor, or of gratitude! Tell me,
for I will know, what devil masked she was, you were with
at the play yesterday.

DORIMANT.

Faith, I resolved as much as you, but the devil was obstinate
and would not tell me.   150

MRS. LOVEIT.

False in this as in your vows to me! You do know!

DORIMANT.

The truth is, I did all I could to know.

MRS. LOVEIT.

And dare you own it to my face? Hell and furies!

Tears her fan in pieces.

DORIMANT.

Spare your fan, madam. You are growing hot and will want
it to cool you.   155

MRS. LOVEIT.

Horror and distraction seize you! Sorrow and remorse gnaw
your soul and punish all your perjuries to me!   *Weeps.*

DORIMANT (*turning to* Bellinda).

    "So thunder breaks the cloud in twain.
    And makes a passage for the rain."

158. cloud] *Q 1, 1704;* clouds *Q 2–3.*

158–159. *So . . . rain*] Matthew Roydon, "An Elegy, or Friend's Passion,
for his Astrophill," ll. 59–60; identified by R. G. Howarth, "Untraced
Quotations in Etherege," *Notes and Queries,* CLXXXVIII (June, 1945),
281. Roydon's elegy for Sir Philip Sidney was published in *The Phoenix Nest*
(1593). Dorimant substitutes *breaks* for the original "rends."

(*To* Bellinda.)   Bellinda, you are the devil that have raised 160
this storm. You were at the play yesterday and have been
making discoveries to your dear.

BELLINDA.

Y'are the most mistaken man i' the world.

DORIMANT.

It must be so, and here I vow revenge—resolve to pursue
and persecute you more impertinently than ever any loving 165
fop did his mistress, hunt you i' the Park, trace you i' the
Mail, dog you in every visit you make, haunt you at the
plays and i' the drawing room, hang my nose in your neck
and talk to you whether you will or no, and ever look upon
you with such dying eyes till your friends grow jealous of 170
me, send you out of town, and the world suspect your reputation. (*In a lower voice.*)   At my Lady Townley's when
we go from hence.

He looks kindly on Bellinda.

BELLINDA.

I'll meet you there.

DORIMANT.

Enough.   175

MRS. LOVEIT (*pushing* Dorimant *away*).

Stand off! You sha' not stare upon her so.

DORIMANT.

Good, there's one made jealous already.

MRS. LOVEIT.

Is this the constancy you vowed?

DORIMANT.

Constancy at my years? 'Tis not a virtue in season; you
might as well expect the fruit the autumn ripens i' the 180
spring.

MRS. LOVEIT.

Monstrous principle!

DORIMANT.

Youth has a long journey to go, madam. Should I have set

171. and the] *Q1–3; and make the*   177. there's] *Q1–2, 1704;* there is
1704.   *Q3.*

---

166. *the Park*] either Hyde Park or St. James's Park, both fashionable.
166–167. *the Mail*] the Mall, a walk bordering St. James's Park.
183–184. *set . . . rest*] taken residence.

up my rest at the first inn I lodged at, I should never have
arrived at the happiness I now enjoy.   185

MRS. LOVEIT.

Dissembler, damned dissembler!

DORIMANT.

I am so, I confess. Good nature and good manners corrupt
me. I am honest in my inclinations and would not, wer't not
to avoid offense, make a lady a little in years believe I think
her young, wilfully mistake art for nature, and seem as fond 190
of a thing I am weary of as when I doted on't in earnest.

MRS. LOVEIT.

False man!

DORIMANT.

True woman.

MRS. LOVEIT.

Now you begin to show yourself.

DORIMANT.

Love gilds us over and makes us show fine things to one 195
another for a time; but soon the gold wears off, and then
again the native brass appears.

MRS. LOVEIT.

Think on your oaths, your vows, and protestations, perjured
man!

DORIMANT.

I made 'em when I was in love.   200

MRS. LOVEIT.

And therefore ought they not to bind? Oh, impious!

DORIMANT.

What we swear at such a time may be a certain proof of a
present passion; but to say truth, in love there is no security
to be given for the future.

MRS. LOVEIT.

Horrid and ungrateful, begone! And never see me more!   205

DORIMANT.

I am not one of those troublesome coxcombs who, because
they were once well-received, take the privilege to plague a
woman with their love ever after. I shall obey you, madam,
though I do myself some violence.

191. of as] Q 2–3; off as Q 1, 1704.

He offers to go, and Mrs. Loveit *pulls him back.*

MRS. LOVEIT.

Come back, you sha' not go! Could you have the ill nature 210
to offer it?

DORIMANT.

When love grows diseased, the best thing we can do is to put
it to a violent death. I cannot endure the torture of a ling'-
ring and consumptive passion.

MRS. LOVEIT.

Can you think mine sickly?   215

DORIMANT.

Oh, 'tis desperately ill! What worse symptoms are there
than your being always uneasy when I visit you, your
picking quarrels with me on slight occasions, and in my
absence kindly list'ning to the impertinences of every
fashionable fool that talks to you?   220

MRS. LOVEIT.

What fashionable fool can you lay to my charge?

DORIMANT.

Why, the very cock-fool of all those fools, Sir Fopling
Flutter.

MRS. LOVEIT.

I never saw him in my life but once.

DORIMANT.

The worse woman you, at first sight to put on all your 225
charms, to entertain him with that softness in your voice
and all that wanton kindness in your eyes you so notoriously
affect when you design a conquest.

MRS. LOVEIT.

So damned a lie did never malice yet invent. Who told you
this?   230

DORIMANT.

No matter. That ever I should love a woman that can dote
on a senseless caper, a tawdry French ribbon, and a formal
cravat!

MRS. LOVEIT.

You make me mad!

219. impertinences] *Q 1-3;* imper-   229. never malice] *Q 1, 1704;* mal-
tinencies *1704.*   ice never *Q 2-3.*

DORIMANT.

> A guilty conscience may do much. Go on, be the game- 235
> mistress of the town and enter all our young fops, as fast as
> they come from travel.

MRS. LOVEIT.

> Base and scurrilous!

DORIMANT.

> A fine mortifying reputation 'twill be for a woman of your
> pride, wit, and quality!   240

MRS. LOVEIT.

> This jealousy's a mere pretense, a cursed trick of your own
> devising. I know you.

DORIMANT.

> Believe it and all the ill of me you can. I would not have a
> woman have the least good thought of me that can think
> well of Fopling. Farewell. Fall to, and much good may do 245
> you with your coxcomb.

MRS. LOVEIT.

> Stay! Oh stay, and I will tell you all.

DORIMANT.

> I have been told too much already.

Exit Dorimant.

MRS. LOVEIT.

> Call him again!

PERT.

> E'en let him go. A fair riddance!   250

MRS. LOVEIT.

> Run, I say, call him again. I will have him called!

PERT.

> The devil should carry him away first, were it my concern.

Exit Pert.

BELLINDA.

> H'as frighted me from the very thoughts of loving men.
> For heav'n's sake, my dear, do not discover what I told you.
> I dread his tongue as much as you ought to have done his 255
> friendship.

---

245. to] *Q2-3, 1704;* too *Q1.*   253. H'as] *Q1-2, 1704;* He 'as *Q3.*

---

236. *enter*] train, initiate.
245-246. *much . . . you*] conventional idiom, usually ironic.
250. *E'en*] intensive, roughly equivalent to "just."

Enter Pert.

PERT.

He's gone, madam.

MRS. LOVEIT.

Lightning blast him!

PERT.

When I told him you desired him to come back, he smiled,
made a mouth at me, flung into his coach, and said—   260

MRS. LOVEIT.

What did he say?

PERT.

"Drive away"; and then repeated verses.

MRS. LOVEIT.

Would I had made a contract to be a witch when first I
entertained this greater devil. Monster, barbarian! I could
tear myself in pieces. Revenge, nothing but revenge can   265
ease me. Plague, war, famine, fire, all that can bring universal ruin and misery on mankind—with joy I'd perish to have
you in my power but this moment!   *Exit* Mrs. Loveit.

PERT.

Follow, madam. Leave her not in this outrageous passion.

                          Pert *gathers up the things.*

BELLINDA.

H'as given me the proof which I desired of his love; but 'tis   270
a proof of his ill nature too. I wish I had not seen him use
her so.

         I sigh to think that Dorimant may be
         One day as faithless and unkind to me.   *Exeunt.*

264. greater] *Q 1–3;* great *1704.*   *Brett-Smith print as verse:* "But . . .
270–272. but . . . so] *1704, Verity,*   too;/I . . . so."

ACT III

[III.i]

Lady Woodvill's lodgings. Enter Harriet *and* Busy, *her woman.*

BUSY.

Dear madam, let me set that curl in order.

HARRIET.

Let me alone, I will shake 'em all out of order!

BUSY.

Will you never leave this wildness?

HARRIET.

Torment me not.

BUSY.

Look, there's a knot falling off.   5

HARRIET.

Let it drop.

BUSY.

But one pin, dear madam.

HARRIET.

How do I daily suffer under thy officious fingers!

BUSY.

Ah, the difference that is between you and my Lady
Dapper! How uneasy she is if the least thing be amiss about   10
her!

HARRIET.

She is indeed most exact. Nothing is ever wanting to make
her ugliness remarkable.

BUSY.

Jeering people say so.

HARRIET.

Her powdering, painting, and her patching never fail in   15
public to draw the tongues and eyes of all the men upon her.

BUSY.

She is indeed a little too pretending.

HARRIET.

That women should set up for beauty as much in spite of
nature as some men have done for wit!

---

15. *patching*] It was the fashion for women to wear small patches, usually
of black silk, on the face.

BUSY.

>I hope without offense one may endeavor to make one's self   20
>agreeable.

HARRIET.

>Not when 'tis impossible. Women then ought to be no more
>fond of dressing than fools should be of talking. Hoods and
>modesty, masks and silence, things that shadow and conceal
>—they should think of nothing else.   25

BUSY.

>Jesu, madam! What will your mother think is become of
>you? For heav'n's sake, go in again.

HARRIET.

>I won't.

BUSY.

>This is the extravagant'st thing that ever you did in your
>life, to leave her and a gentleman who is to be your husband.   30

HARRIET.

>My husband! Hast thou so little wit to think I spoke what I
>meant when I overjoyed her in the country with a low
>curtsy and "What you please, madam; I shall ever be
>obedient"?

BUSY.

>Nay, I know not, you have so many fetches.   35

HARRIET.

>And this was one, to get her up to London. Nothing else, I
>assure thee.

BUSY.

>Well! The man, in my mind, is a fine man.

HARRIET.

>The man indeed wears his clothes fashionably and has a
>pretty, negligent way with him, very courtly and much   40
>affected. He bows, and talks, and smiles so agreeably as he
>thinks.

BUSY.

>I never saw anything so genteel.

23. of talking] *Q 1–3; 1704 omits of.*   *Q 1; say Yale copy of Q 1 (reported in*
43. saw] *Q 2–3, 1704, and normally in*   *Nettleton-Case).*

35. *fetches*] tricks.

HARRIET.

Varnished over with good breeding, many a blockhead
makes a tolerable show.   45

BUSY.

I wonder you do not like him.

HARRIET.

I think I might be brought to endure him, and that is all a
reasonable woman should expect in a husband; but there
is duty i' the case, and like the haughty Merab, I
        "Find much aversion in my stubborn mind,"   50
which
        "Is bred by being promised and designed."

BUSY.

I wish you do not design your own ruin. I partly guess your
inclinations, madam. That Mr. Dorimant—

HARRIET.

Leave your prating and sing some foolish song or other.   55

BUSY.

I will—the song you love so well ever since you saw Mr.
Dorimant.

SONG

When first Amintas charmed my heart,
    My heedless sheep began to stray;
The wolves soon stole the greatest part,   60
    And all will now be made a prey.

Ah, let not love your thoughts possess,
    'Tis fatal to a shepherdess;
The dang'rous passion you must shun,
    Or else like me be quite undone.   65

51–52. which . . . designed] *as printed by Brett-Smith. In Q1 the first line
of the couplet concludes p. 32; the
catchword is* which, *but it does not*
*occur on p. 33. Q2–3 and 1704 incor-
porate* which *in the second line of the
couplet:* Which is . . . designed.

49. *Merab*] elder daughter of Saul, promised to David but then married
to Adriel.

50–52. *Find . . . designed*] Harriet alludes to Abraham Cowley's portrayal
of "haughty" Merab in *Davideis*, Book III: "And much aversion in her
stubborn mind/ Was bred by being *promis'd* and *design'd*" (*Poems*, ed. A. R.
Waller [Cambridge, 1905], p. 341).

HARRIET.

Shall I be paid down by a covetous parent for a purchase?
I need no land. No, I'll lay myself out all in love. It is
decreed.

Enter Young Bellair.

YOUNG BELLAIR.

What generous resolution are you making, madam?

HARRIET.

Only to be disobedient, sir.   70

YOUNG BELLAIR.

Let me join hands with you in that.

HARRIET.

With all my heart. I never thought I should have given
you mine so willingly. Here.

[*They join hands.*]

I, Harriet—

YOUNG BELLAIR.

And I, Harry—   75

HARRIET. .

Do solemnly protest—

YOUNG BELLAIR.

And vow—

HARRIET.

That I with you—

YOUNG BELLAIR.

And I with you—

HARRIET. YOUNG BELLAIR.

Will never marry.   80

HARRIET.

A match!

YOUNG BELLAIR.

And no match! How do you like this indifference now?

HARRIET.

You expect I should take it ill, I see.

YOUNG BELLAIR.

'Tis not unnatural for you women to be a little angry, you

84. for you] *Q1, 1704;* for young
Q2-3.

---

67. *lay . . . out*] spend myself.
84–85. *you miss a conquest*] i.e., if you miss a conquest.

miss a conquest—though you would slight the poor man   85
were he in your power.

HARRIET.

There are some, it may be, have an eye like Bart'lomew,
big enough for the whole fair; but I am not of the number,
and you may keep your gingerbread. 'Twill be more
acceptable to the lady whose dear image it wears.   90

YOUNG BELLAIR.

I must confess, madam, you came a day after the fair.

HARRIET.

You own then you are in love?

YOUNG BELLAIR.

I do.

HARRIET.

The confidence is generous, and in return I could almost
find in my heart to let you know my inclinations.   95

YOUNG BELLAIR.

Are you in love?

HARRIET.

Yes—with this dear town, to that degree I can scarce
endure the country in landscapes and in hangings.

YOUNG BELLAIR.

What a dreadful thing 'twould be to be hurried back to
Hampshire!   100

HARRIET.

Ah, name it not.

YOUNG BELLAIR.

As for us, I find we shall agree well enough. Would we could
do something to deceive the grave people!

HARRIET.

Could we delay their quick proceeding, 'twere well. A
reprieve is a good step towards the getting of a pardon.   105

104. quick] *Q 1–3; 1704 omits.*

87–88. *an eye . . . fair*] referring to the extravagance of Bartholomew
Cokes in Ben Jonson's *Bartholomew Fair*, Act III. The fair was held to
coincide with St. Bartholomew's day (August 24th) in the suburb of
Smithfield.

89. *gingerbread*] staple item at the fair, then as now shaped into human
figures, letters, etc.

91. *you . . . fair*] proverbial.

98. *hangings*] tapestries, wallpaper, etc.

YOUNG BELLAIR.

If we give over the game, we are undone. What think you of playing it on booty?

HARRIET.

What do you mean?

YOUNG BELLAIR.

Pretend to be in love with one another. 'Twill make some dilatory excuses we may feign pass the better.   110

HARRIET.

Let us do 't, if it be but for the dear pleasure of dissembling.

YOUNG BELLAIR.

Can you play your part?

HARRIET.

I know not what it is to love, but I have made pretty remarks by being now and then where lovers meet. Where did you leave their gravities?   115

YOUNG BELLAIR.

I' th' next room. Your mother was censuring our modern gallant.

Enter Old Bellair *and* Lady Woodvill.

HARRIET.

Peace, here they come. I will lean against this wall and look bashfully down upon my fan while you, like an amorous spark, modishly entertain me.   120

LADY WOODVILL [*to* Old Bellair].

Never go about to excuse 'em. Come, come, it was not so when I was a young woman.

OLD BELLAIR.

Adod, they're something disrespectful—

LADY WOODVILL.

Quality was then considered and not rallied by every fleering fellow.   125

OLD BELLAIR.

Youth will have its jest, adod it will.

113. it is] *Q1–3;* 'tis *1704.*   118. I will] *Q1–2, 1704;* I'll *Q3.*

---

107. *playing . . . booty*] conspiring to victimize other players.
114. *remarks*] observations.
125. *fleering*] impudent, jeering.

LADY WOODVILL.

'Tis good breeding now to be civil to none but players and
Exchange women. They are treated by 'em as much above
their condition as others are below theirs.

OLD BELLAIR.

Out, a pize on 'em! Talk no more; the rogues ha' got an ill 130
habit of preferring beauty, no matter where they find it.

LADY WOODVILL.

See your son and my daughter. They have improved their
acquaintance since they were within.

OLD BELLAIR.

Adod, methinks they have! Let's keep back and observe.

YOUNG BELLAIR [*to* Harriet].

Now for a look and gestures that may persuade 'em I am 135
saying all the passionate things imaginable.

HARRIET.

Your head a little more on one side. Ease yourself on your
left leg and play with your right hand.

YOUNG BELLAIR.

Thus, is it not?

HARRIET.

Now set your right leg firm on the ground, adjust your belt, 140
then look about you.

YOUNG BELLAIR.

A little exercising will make me perfect.

HARRIET.

Smile, and turn to me again very sparkish.

YOUNG BELLAIR.

Will you take your turn and be instructed?

HARRIET.

With all my heart.   145

YOUNG BELLAIR.

At one motion play your fan, roll your eyes, and then
settle a kind look upon me.

HARRIET.

So.

127. be] *Q 1–3; 1704 omits.*   135. I am] *Q 1, 1704;* I'm *Q 2–3.*

` 128. *Exchange women*] shopwomen at the New Exchange.

YOUNG BELLAIR.

Now spread your fan, look down upon it, and tell the sticks
with a finger.   150

HARRIET.

Very modish.

YOUNG BELLAIR.

Clap your hand up to your bosom, hold down your gown.
Shrug a little, draw up your breasts and let 'em fall again,
gently, with a sigh or two, *etc.*

HARRIET.

By the good instructions you give, I suspect you for one of 155
those malicious observers who watch people's eyes, and
from innocent looks make scandalous conclusions.

YOUNG BELLAIR.

I know some, indeed, who out of mere love to mischief are
as vigilant as jealousy itself, and will give you an account of
every glance that passes at a play and i' th' Circle.   160

HARRIET.

'Twill not be amiss now to seem a little pleasant.

YOUNG BELLAIR.

Clap your fan then in both your hands, snatch it to your
mouth, smile, and with a lively motion fling your body a
little forwards. So! Now spread it, fall back on the sudden,
cover your face with it, and break out into a loud laughter. 165
—Take up! Look grave and fall a-fanning of yourself.
Admirably well acted!

HARRIET.

I think I am pretty apt at these matters.

OLD BELLAIR [*to* Lady Woodvill].

Adod, I like this well.

LADY WOODVILL.

This promises something.   170

OLD BELLAIR [*coming forward*].

Come, there is love i' th' case, adod there is, or will be.
—What say you, young lady?

171. i' th'] *Q1–2, 1704;* in the *Q3.*

---

154. *etc.*] S.D.; the actors were, evidently, to improvise.
160. *th' Circle*] the Ring, a circular path in Hyde Park for riding and
walking; or, possibly, the assembly at court (cf. IV.i.126).

HARRIET.

All in good time, sir. You expect we should fall to and love as gamecocks fight, as soon as we are set together. Adod, y'are unreasonable!   175

OLD BELLAIR.

Adod, sirrah, I like thy wit well.

Enter a Servant.

SERVANT.

The coach is at the door, madam.

OLD BELLAIR.

Go, get you and take the air together.

LADY WOODVILL.

Will not you go with us?

OLD BELLAIR.

Out a pize! Adod, I ha' business and cannot. We shall meet 180 at night at my sister Townley's.

YOUNG BELLAIR (*aside*).

He's going to Emilia. I overheard him talk of a collation.

Exeunt.

[III.ii]

[*Lady Townley's.*] *Enter* Lady Townley, Emilia, *and* Medley.

LADY TOWNLEY.

I pity the young lovers we last talked of, though to say truth, their conduct has been so indiscreet they deserve to be unfortunate.

MEDLEY.

Y' have an exact account, from the great lady i' th' box down to the little orange-wench.   5

EMILIA.

Y'are a living libel, a breathing lampoon. I wonder you are not torn in pieces.

MEDLEY.

What think you of setting up an office of intelligence for these matters? The project may get money.

LADY TOWNLEY.

You would have great dealings with country ladies.   10

10. would] *Q 1–2, 1704;* will *Q 3.*

MEDLEY.

    More than Muddiman has with their husbands!

Enter Bellinda.

LADY TOWNLEY.

    Bellinda, what has been become of you? We have not seen
you here of late with your friend Mrs. Loveit.

BELLINDA.

    Dear creature, I left her but now so sadly afflicted.

LADY TOWNLEY.

    With her old distemper, jealousy?   15

MEDLEY.

    Dorimant has played her some new prank.

BELLINDA.

    Well, that Dorimant is certainly the worst man breathing.

EMILIA.

    I once thought so.

BELLINDA.

    And do you not think so still?

EMILIA.

    No, indeed.   20

BELLINDA.

    Oh, Jesu!

EMILIA.

    The town does him a great deal of injury, and I will never
believe what it says of a man I do not know, again, for his
sake.

BELLINDA.

    You make me wonder.   25

LADY TOWNLEY.

    He's a very well-bred man.

BELLINDA.

    But strangely ill-natured.

EMILIA.

    Then he's a very witty man.

BELLINDA.

    But a man of no principles.

14. her] *Q1–3; 1704 omits.*

---

11. *Muddiman*] Henry Muddiman (1629–1692); journalist and author of
a popular newsletter.

MEDLEY.

    Your man of principles is a very fine thing, indeed!   30

BELLINDA.

    To be preferred to men of parts by women who have regard
to their reputation and quiet. Well, were I minded to play
the fool, he should be the last man I'd think of.

MEDLEY.

    He has been the first in many ladies' favors, though you are
so severe, madam.   35

LADY TOWNLEY.

    What he may be for a lover, I know not; but he's a very
pleasant acquaintance, I am sure.

BELLINDA.

    Had you seen him use Mrs. Loveit as I have done, you
would never endure him more.

EMILIA.

    What, he has quarreled with her again?   40

BELLINDA.

    Upon the slightest occasion. He's jealous of Sir Fopling.

LADY TOWNLEY.

    She never saw him in her life but yesterday; and that was
here.

EMILIA.

    On my conscience, he's the only man in town that's her
aversion. How horribly out of humor she was all the while 45
he talked to her!

BELLINDA.

    And somebody has wickedly told him—

Enter Dorimant.

EMILIA.

    Here he comes.

MEDLEY.

    Dorimant, you are luckily come to justify yourself. Here's a
lady—   50

BELLINDA.

    —Has a word or two to say to you from a disconsolate
person.

DORIMANT.

    You tender your reputation too much, I know, madam, to
whisper with me before this good company.

BELLINDA.

  To serve Mrs. Loveit, I'll make a bold venture.   55

DORIMANT.

  Here's Medley, the very spirit of scandal.

BELLINDA.

  No matter.

EMILIA.

  'Tis something you are unwilling to hear, Mr. Dorimant.

LADY TOWNLEY.

  Tell him, Bellinda, whether he will or no.

BELLINDA (*aloud*).

  Mrs. Loveit—   60

DORIMANT.

  Softly, these are laughers; you do not know 'em.

BELLINDA (*to* Dorimant, *apart*).

  In a word, y'ave made me hate you, which I thought you
  never could have done.

DORIMANT.

  In obeying your commands?

BELLINDA.

  'Twas a cruel part you played. How could you act it?   65

DORIMANT.

  Nothing is cruel to a man who could kill himself to please
  you. Remember, five o'clock tomorrow morning.

BELLINDA.

  I tremble when you name it.

DORIMANT.

  Be sure you come.

BELLINDA.

  I sha' not.   70

DORIMANT.

  Swear you will.

BELLINDA.

  I dare not.

DORIMANT.

  Swear, I say!

BELLINDA.

  By my life, by all the happiness I hope for—

DORIMANT.

  You will.   75

58. you] *Q1, Q3, 1704;* your *Q2.*

BELLINDA.
I will.

DORIMANT.
Kind.

BELLINDA.
I am glad I've sworn. I vow I think I should have failed
you else.

DORIMANT.
Surprisingly kind! In what temper did you leave Loveit?   80

BELLINDA.
Her raving was prettily over, and she began to be in a
brave way of defying you and all your works. Where have
you been since you went from thence?

DORIMANT.
I looked in at the play.

BELLINDA.
I have promised and must return to her again.   85

DORIMANT.
Persuade her to walk in the Mail this evening.

BELLINDA.
She hates the place and will not come.

DORIMANT.
Do all you can to prevail with her.

BELLINDA.
For what purpose?

DORIMANT.
Sir Fopling will be here anon. I'll prepare him to set upon   90
her there before me.

BELLINDA.
You persecute her too much. But I'll do all you'll ha' me.

DORIMANT (*aloud*).
Tell her plainly, 'tis grown so dull a business I can drudge
on no longer.

EMILIA.
There are afflictions in love, Mr. Dorimant.   95

DORIMANT.
You women make 'em, who are commonly as unreasonable
in that as you are at play: without the advantage be on your
side, a man can never quietly give over when he's weary.

---

81. *prettily*] almost.

MEDLEY.

If you would play without being obliged to complaisance,
Dorimant, you should play in public places.   100

DORIMANT.

Ordinaries were a very good thing for that, but gentlemen
do not of late frequent 'em. The deep play is now in private
houses.

Bellinda *offering to steal away.*

LADY TOWNLEY.

Bellinda, are you leaving us so soon?

BELLINDA.

I am to go to the Park with Mrs. Loveit, madam.   105

Exit Bellinda.

LADY TOWNLEY.

This confidence will go nigh to spoil this young creature.

MEDLEY.

'Twill do her good, madam. Young men who are brought
up under practicing lawyers prove the abler counsel when
they come to be called to the bar themselves.

DORIMANT.

The town has been very favorable to you this afternoon, my   110
Lady Townley. You use to have an *embarras* of chairs and
coaches at your door, an uproar of footmen in your hall, and
a noise of fools above here.

LADY TOWNLEY.

Indeed, my house is the general rendezvous and, next to
the playhouse, is the common refuge of all the young idle   115
people.

EMILIA.

Company is a very good thing, madam, but I wonder you do
not love it a little more chosen.

LADY TOWNLEY.

'Tis good to have an universal taste. We should love wit, but

---

101. *Ordinaries*] taverns.
106. *This confidence*] i.e., Loveit's and Dorimant's "confiding" in
Bellinda.
111–112. *embarras . . . coaches*] Cf. *embarras de voitures* (Fr.), a congestion
of carriages; "traffic jam."

for variety be able to divert ourselves with the extravagan-   120
cies of those who want it.

MEDLEY.

Fools will make you laugh.

EMILIA.

For once or twice; but the repetition of their folly after a
visit or two grows tedious and insufferable.

LADY TOWNLEY.

You are a little too delicate, Emilia.   125

Enter a Page.

PAGE.

Sir Fopling Flutter, madam, desires to know if you are to be
seen.

LADY TOWNLEY.

Here's the freshest fool in town, and one who has not cloyed
you yet.—Page!

PAGE.

Madam?   130

LADY TOWNLEY.

Desire him to walk up.   [*Exit* Page.]

DORIMANT.

Do not you fall on him, Medley, and snub him. Soothe him
up in his extravagance. He will show the better.

MEDLEY.

You know I have a natural indulgence for fools and need
not this caution, sir.   135

Enter Sir Fopling, *with his Page after him.*

SIR FOPLING.

Page, wait without.   [*Exit Page.*]
(*To* Lady Townley.)   Madam, I kiss your hands. I see yesterday was nothing of chance; the *belles assemblées* form
themselves here every day. (*To* Emilia.) Lady, your
servant.—Dorimant, let me embrace thee. Without lying,   140
I have not met with any of my acquaintance who retain so
much of Paris as thou dost—the very air thou hadst when

123. the] *Q1–2, 1704;* a *Q3.*

---

138. *belles assemblées*] fashionable gatherings.

the marquise mistook thee i' th' Tuileries and cried "Hé, chevalier!" and then begged thy pardon.

DORIMANT.

I would fain wear in fashion as long as I can, sir. 'Tis a 145 thing to be valued in men as well as baubles.

SIR FOPLING.

Thou art a man of wit and understands the town. Prithee let thee and I be intimate. There is no living without making some good man the confidant of our pleasures.

DORIMANT.

'Tis true; but there is no man so improper for such a 150 business as I am.

SIR FOPLING.

Prithee, why hast thou so modest an opinion of thyself?

DORIMANT.

Why, first, I could never keep a secret in my life; and then, there is no charm so infallibly makes me fall in love with a woman as my knowing a friend loves her. I deal honestly 155 with you.

SIR FOPLING.

Thy humor's very gallant, or let me perish. I knew a French count so like thee.

LADY TOWNLEY.

Wit, I perceive, has more power over you than beauty, Sir Fopling, else you would not have let this lady stand so long 160 neglected.

SIR FOPLING (to Emilia).

A thousand pardons, madam. Some civility's due of course upon the meeting a long absent friend. The *éclat* of so much beauty, I confess, ought to have charmed me sooner.

EMILIA.

The *brillant* of so much good language, sir, has much more 165 power than the little beauty I can boast.

SIR FOPLING.

I never saw anything prettier than this high work on your

147. understands] *Q1–3;* understand'st *1704.*

---

143. *th' Tuileries*] gardens of the *Palais des Tuileries* in Paris.
163. *éclat*] sparkle.   165. *brillant*] glitter.

point d'Espaigne.

EMILIA.

'Tis not so rich as *point de Venise.*

SIR FOPLING.

Not altogether, but looks cooler, and is more proper for the　170
season. —Dorimant, is not that Medley?

DORIMANT.

The same, sir.

SIR FOPLING [*to* Medley].

Forgive me, sir; in this *embarras* of civilities I could not come
to have you in my arms sooner. You understand an equipage
the best of any man in town, I hear.　　　　175

MEDLEY.

By my own you would not guess it.

SIR FOPLING.

There are critics who do not write, sir.

MEDLEY.

Our peevish poets will scarce allow it.

SIR FOPLING.

Damn 'em, they'll allow no man wit who does not play the
fool like themselves and show it! Have you taken notice of　180
the gallesh I brought over?

MEDLEY.

Oh, yes! 'T has quite another air than th' English makes.

SIR FOPLING.

'Tis as easily known from an English tumbril as an Inns of
Court man is from one of us.

DORIMANT.

Truly there is a *bel air* in galleshes as well as men.　　　185

MEDLEY.

But there are few so delicate to observe it.

182. 'T has] *Q1–3;* It has *1704.*　　　182. th'] *Q1–2, 1704;* the *Q3.*

---

168. *point d'Espaigne*] Spanish lace.
169. *point de Venise*] Venetian lace.
174. *equipage*] retinue.
181. *gallesh*] *calèche* (Fr.); light carriage with a folding top.
183. *tumbril*] cart that tilts to empty its load; especially, a dung cart.
183–184. *Inns of Court man*] lawyer; the Inns of Court are legal societies.
185. *bel air*] fashionable style.

SIR FOPLING.

   The world is generally very *grossier* here, indeed.

LADY TOWNLEY [*to* Emilia].

   He's very fine.

EMILIA.

   Extreme proper!

SIR FOPLING.

   A slight suit I made to appear in at my first arrival—not   190
   worthy your consideration, ladies.

DORIMANT.

   The pantaloon is very well mounted.

SIR FOPLING.

   The tassels are new and pretty.

MEDLEY.

   I never saw a coat better cut.

SIR FOPLING.

   It makes me show long-waisted, and I think slender.   195

DORIMANT.

   That's the shape our ladies dote on.

MEDLEY.

   Your breech, though, is a handful too high, in my eye, Sir
   Fopling.

SIR FOPLING.

   Peace, Medley, I have wished it lower a thousand times; but
   a pox on't, 'twill not be!   200

LADY TOWNLEY.

   His gloves are well fringed, large and graceful.

SIR FOPLING.

   I was always eminent for being *bien ganté.*

EMILIA.

   He wears nothing but what are originals of the most famous
   hands in Paris.

SIR FOPLING.

   You are in the right, madam.   205

LADY TOWNLEY.

   The suit?

---

187. *grossier*] crude.
202. *bien ganté*] well-gloved.

SIR FOPLING.
    Barroy.

EMILIA.
    The garniture?

SIR FOPLING.
    Le Gras.

MEDLEY.
    The shoes?   210

SIR FOPLING.
    Piccar.

DORIMANT.
    The periwig?

SIR FOPLING.
    Chedreux.

LADY TOWNLEY. EMILIA.
    The gloves?

SIR FOPLING.
    Orangerie. You know the smell, ladies. —Dorimant, I could 215
    find in my heart for an amusement to have a gallantry with
    some of our English ladies.

DORIMANT.
    'Tis a thing no less necessary to confirm the reputation of
    your wit than a duel will be to satisfy the town of your
    courage.   220

SIR FOPLING.
    Here was a woman yesterday—

DORIMANT.
    Mrs. Loveit.

SIR FOPLING.
    You have named her!

DORIMANT.
    You cannot pitch on a better for your purpose.

222. Mrs.] *Q3; Q1–2, 1704 print*
Mistress.

---

207. *Barroy*] Sir Fopling lists a series of Parisian merchants; Chedreux
(1. 213, below) is remembered as giving his name to a modish style of wig.
208. *garniture*] trimmings.
215. *Orangerie*] i.e., scented with orange.

SIR FOPLING.

    Prithee, what is she?   225

DORIMANT.

    A person of quality, and one who has a rest of reputation
enough to make the conquest considerable. Besides, I hear
she likes you too.

SIR FOPLING.

    Methoughts she seemed, though, very reserved and uneasy
all the time I entertained her.   230

DORIMANT.

    Grimace and affectation! You will see her i' th' Mail
tonight.

SIR FOPLING.

    Prithee, let thee and I take the air together.

DORIMANT.

    I am engaged to Medley, but I'll meet you at Saint James's
and give you some information upon the which you may 235
regulate your proceedings.

SIR FOPLING.

    All the world will be in the Park tonight. —Ladies, 'twere
pity to keep so much beauty longer within doors and rob the
Ring of all those charms that should adorn it. —Hey, page!

Enter Page.

    See that all my people be ready.   [*Page*] *goes out again.* 240
    Dorimant, *au revoir.*   [*Exit* Sir Fopling.]

MEDLEY.

    A fine-mettled coxcomb.

DORIMANT.

    Brisk and insipid.

MEDLEY.

    Pert and dull.

EMILIA.

    However you despise him, gentlemen, I'll lay my life he 245
passes for a wit with many.

---

231. affectation] *Q 1–3;* affection   231. th'] *Q 1–2, 1704;* the *Q 3.*
1704.   237. be] *Q 1, Q 3, 1704; Q 2 omits.*

226–227. *a rest . . . enough*] enough reputation left.
238–239. *the Ring*] see III.i.160 n.

DORIMANT.

That may very well be. Nature has her cheats, stums a brain, and puts sophisticate dullness often on the tasteless multitude for true wit and good humor. —Medley, come.

MEDLEY.

I must go a little way; I will meet you i' the Mail.   250

DORIMANT.

I'll walk through the garden thither. (*To the women.*) We shall meet anon and bow.

LADY TOWNLEY.

Not tonight. We are engaged about a business, the knowledge of which may make you laugh hereafter.

MEDLEY.

Your servant, ladies.   255

DORIMANT.

Au revoir, as Sir Fopling says.   *Exeunt* Medley *and* Dorimant.

LADY TOWNLEY.

The old man will be here immediately.

EMILIA.

Let's expect him i' th' garden.

LADY TOWNLEY.

Go, you are a rogue!

EMILIA.

I can't abide you!   *Exeunt.* 260

[III.iii]

The Mail. Enter Harriet *and* Young Bellair, *she pulling him.*

HARRIET.

Come along!

YOUNG BELLAIR.

And leave your mother?

HARRIET.

Busy will be sent with a hue and cry after us; but that's no matter.

---

247. *stums*] To *stum* wine is to renew it by raising a new fermentation.
248. *sophisticate*] deceptive.
250. *I . . . way*] i.e., I can't go with you directly.
258. *expect*] wait for.

YOUNG BELLAIR.

'Twill look strangely in me.   5

HARRIET.

She'll believe it a freak of mine and never blame your
manners.

YOUNG BELLAIR [*pointing*].

What reverend acquaintance is that she has met?

HARRIET.

A fellow beauty of the last king's time, though by the ruins
you would hardly guess it.   *Exeunt.*   10

Enter Dorimant *and crosses the stage.*
Enter Young Bellair *and* Harriet.

YOUNG BELLAIR.

By this time your mother is in a fine taking.

HARRIET.

If your friend Mr. Dorimant were but here now, that she
might find me talking with him!

YOUNG BELLAIR.

She does not know him but dreads him, I hear, of all
mankind.   15

HARRIET.

She concludes if he does but speak to a woman, she's undone
—is on her knees every day to pray heav'n defend me from
him.

YOUNG BELLAIR.

You do not apprehend him so much as she does?

HARRIET.

I never saw anything in him that was frightful.   20

YOUNG BELLAIR.

On the contrary, have you not observed something extreme
delightful in his wit and person?

HARRIET.

He's agreeable and pleasant, I must own, but he does so
much affect being so, he displeases me.

YOUNG BELLAIR.

Lord, madam, all he does and says is so easy and so natural.   25

---

9. *the last king's time*] reign of Charles I, more than twenty-five years
before.
11. *in . . . taking*] excited; "in a fine state."

HARRIET.

Some men's verses seem so to the unskilful; but labor i' the one and affectation in the other to the judicious plainly appear.

YOUNG BELLAIR.

I never heard him accused of affectation before.

Enter Dorimant *and stares upon her.*

HARRIET.

It passes on the easy town, who are favorably pleased in   30
him to call it humor.   *Exeunt* Young Bellair *and* Harriet.

DORIMANT.

'Tis she! It must be she—that lovely hair, that easy shape, those wanton eyes, and all those melting charms about her mouth which Medley spoke of. I'll follow the lottery and put in for a prize with my friend Bellair.   35

Exit Dorimant, *repeating:*
"In love the victors from the vanquished fly;
They fly that wound, and they pursue that die."

Enter Young Bellair *and* Harriet; *and after them* Dorimant, *standing at a distance.*

YOUNG BELLAIR.

Most people prefer High Park to this place.

HARRIET.

It has the better reputation, I confess; but I abominate the dull diversions there—the formal bows, the affected smiles,   40
the silly by-words and amorous tweers in passing. Here one meets with a little conversation now and then.

YOUNG BELLAIR.

These conversations have been fatal to some of your sex, madam.

HARRIET.

It may be so. Because some who want temper have been   45

27. in] *Q 1, 1704;* i' *Q 2-3.*

---

34. *the lottery*] Lotteries were a common means of raising money, both for individuals and for the state.
36-37. *In . . . die*] Waller, "To a Friend, of the Different Success of their Loves," ll. 27-28 (Thorn Drury, I, 103).
38. *High Park*] Hyde Park.
41. *tweers*] glances, leers.   45. *temper*] control.

undone by gaming, must others who have it wholly deny
themselves the pleasure of play?

DORIMANT (*coming up gently and bowing to her*).

Trust me, it were unreasonable, madam.

She starts and looks grave.

HARRIET.

Lord, who's this?

YOUNG BELLAIR.

Dorimant.   50

DORIMANT.

Is this the woman your father would have you marry?

YOUNG BELLAIR.

It is.

DORIMANT.

Her name?

YOUNG BELLAIR.

Harriet.

DORIMANT [*aside*].

I am not mistaken. —She's handsome.   55

YOUNG BELLAIR.

Talk to her; her wit is better than her face. We were wishing
for you but now.

DORIMANT (*to* Harriet).

Overcast with seriousness o' the sudden! A thousand smiles
were shining in that face but now. I never saw so quick a
change of weather.   60

HARRIET (*aside*).

I feel as great a change within, but he shall never know it.

DORIMANT.

You were talking of play, madam. Pray, what may be your
stint?

HARRIET.

A little harmless discourse in public walks or at most an
appointment in a box, barefaced, at the playhouse. You are   65
for masks and private meetings, where women engage for
all they are worth, I hear.

---

63. *stint*] fixed limit.

DORIMANT.

I have been used to deep play, but I can make one at small
game when I like my gamester well.

HARRIET.

And be so unconcerned you'll ha' no pleasure in't.   70

DORIMANT.

Where there is a considerable sum to be won, the hope of
drawing people in makes every trifle considerable.

HARRIET.

The sordidness of men's natures, I know, makes 'em willing
to flatter and comply with the rich, though they are sure
never to be the better for 'em.   75

DORIMANT.

'Tis in their power to do us good, and we despair not but at
some time or other they may be willing.

HARRIET.

To men who have fared in this town like you, 'twould be a
great mortification to live on hope. Could you keep a Lent
for a mistress?   80

DORIMANT.

In expectation of a happy Easter; and though time be very
precious, think forty days well lost to gain your favor.

HARRIET.

Mr. Bellair! Let us walk, 'tis time to leave him. Men grow
dull when they begin to be particular.

DORIMANT.

Y'are mistaken: flattery will not ensue, though I know   85
y'are greedy of the praises of the whole Mail.

HARRIET.

You do me wrong.

DORIMANT.

I do not. As I followed you, I observed how you were pleased
when the fops cried "She's handsome, very handsome, by
God she is!" and whispered aloud your name—the thousand   90
several forms you put your face into; then, to make yourself
more agreeable, how wantonly you played with your head,
flung back your locks, and looked smilingly over your
shoulder at 'em.

70. in't] *Q1–3;* in it *1704.*   78. in] *Q1–3;* on *1704.*

HARRIET.

I do not go begging the men's, as you do the ladies' good   95
liking, with a sly softness in your looks and a gentle slowness
in your bows as you pass by 'em. As thus, sir.   (*Acts him.*)
Is not this like you?

Enter Lady Woodvill *and* Busy.

YOUNG BELLAIR.

Your mother, madam!

Pulls Harriet. *She composes herself.*

LADY WOODVILL.

Ah, my dear child Harriet!   100

BUSY [*aside*].

Now is she so pleased with finding her again, she cannot
chide her.

LADY WOODVILL.

Come away!

DORIMANT.

'Tis now but high Mail, madam—the most entertaining
time of all the evening.   105

HARRIET.

I would fain see that Dorimant, mother, you so cry out of
for a monster. He's in the Mail, I hear.

LADY WOODVILL.

Come away, then! The plague is here, and you should dread
the infection.

YOUNG BELLAIR.

You may be misinformed of the gentleman.   110

LADY WOODVILL.

Oh, no! I hope you do not know him. He is the prince of all
the devils in the town—delights in nothing but in rapes and
riots.

DORIMANT.

If you did but hear him speak, madam—

97. pass] *Q1–2, 1704;* passed *Q3.*   106–107. cry . . . monster] *Q1–3,*
                                          1704; cry out for a monster *D, Verity.*

104. *high Mail*] busiest and most fashionable hour on the Mall.

LADY WOODVILL.

Oh, he has a tongue, they say, would tempt the angels to a 115
second fall.

Enter Sir Fopling *with his equipage, six footmen and a page.*

SIR FOPLING.

Hey, Champagne, Norman, La Rose, La Fleur, La Tour,
La Verdure!—Dorimant!—

LADY WOODVILL.

Here, here he is among this rout! He names him! Come
away, Harriet, come away!   120

Exeunt Lady Woodvill, Harriet, Busy, *and* Young Bellair.

DORIMANT.

This fool's coming has spoiled all: she's gone. But she has
left a pleasing image of herself behind that wanders in my
soul. It must not settle there.

SIR FOPLING.

What reverie is this? Speak, man.

DORIMANT.   "Snatched from myself, how far behind   125
             Already I behold the shore!"

Enter Medley.

MEDLEY.

Dorimant, a discovery! I met with Bellair—

DORIMANT.

You can tell me no news, sir. I know all.

MEDLEY.

How do you like the daughter?

DORIMANT.

You never came so near truth in your life as you did in her 130
description.

MEDLEY.

What think you of the mother?

DORIMANT.

Whatever I think of her, she thinks very well of me, I find.

118. Verdure] *Q 1–3;* Verdue *1704.*   125. Snatched] *Q 1, 1704;* Snatch
                                            Q 2–3.

125–126. *Snatched . . . shore*] Waller, "Of Loving at First Sight," ll. 3–4
(Thorn Drury, I, 100).

MEDLEY.

> Did she know you?

DORIMANT.

> She did not. Whether she does now or no, I know not. Here 135
> was a pleasant scene towards, when in came Sir Fopling,
> mustering up his equipage, and at the latter end named me
> and frighted her away.

MEDLEY.

> Loveit and Bellinda are not far off. I saw 'em alight at St.
> James's. 140

DORIMANT.

> Sir Fopling, hark you, a word or two. (*Whispers*). Look
> you do not want assurance.

SIR FOPLING.

> I never do on these occasions.

DORIMANT.

> Walk on; we must not be seen together. Make your advan-
> tage of what I have told you. The next turn you will meet 145
> the lady.

SIR FOPLING.

> Hey! Follow me all.   *Exeunt* Sir Fopling *and his equipage.*

DORIMANT.

> Medley, you shall see good sport anon between Loveit and
> this Fopling.

MEDLEY.

> I thought there was something toward, by that whisper. 150

DORIMANT.

> You know a worthy principle of hers?

MEDLEY.

> Not to be so much as civil to a man who speaks to her in the
> presence of him she professes to love.

DORIMANT.

> I have encouraged Fopling to talk to her tonight.

139. off] *Q 1–2, 1704; of Q 3.*

---

136. *towards*] in prospect.

139–140. *St. James's*] in this case, probably St. James's Palace, opposite
the park to the west end of the Mall.

145. *The next turn*] i.e., Sir Fopling will walk to the end of the Mall,
then turn back.

MEDLEY.

Now you are here, she will go nigh to beat him.   155

DORIMANT.

In the humor she's in, her love will make her do some very
extravagant thing, doubtless.

MEDLEY.

What was Bellinda's business with you at my Lady
Townley's?

DORIMANT.

To get me to meet Loveit here in order to an *éclaircissement.* 160
I made some difficulty of it and have prepared this rencounter to make good my jealousy.

Enter Mrs. Loveit, Bellinda, *and* Pert.

MEDLEY.

Here they come.

DORIMANT.

I'll meet her and provoke her with a deal of dumb civility
in passing by, then turn short and be behind her when Sir 165
Fopling sets upon her.

[*Bows to Mrs. Loveit.*]

"See how unregarded now
That piece of beauty passes."

Exeunt Dorimant *and* Medley.

BELLINDA.

How wonderful respectfully he bowed!

PERT.

He's always over-mannerly when he has done a mischief.   170

BELLINDA.

Methoughts, indeed, at the same time he had a strange,
despising countenance.

PERT.

The unlucky look he thinks becomes him.

169. respectfully] *Q1-2, 1704;* re-
spectful *Q3.*

---

160. *éclaircissement*] understanding.
161-162. *rencounter*] encounter.
167-168. *See . . . passes*] John Suckling, "Sonnet I," ll. 1-2. Dorimant
substitutes *See* for the original "Do'st see."
173. *unlucky*] mischievous, malicious.

BELLINDA.

I was afraid you would have spoke to him, my dear.

MRS. LOVEIT.

I would have died first. He shall no more find me the loving 175
fool he has done.

BELLINDA.

You love him still!

MRS. LOVEIT.

No.

PERT.

I wish you did not.

MRS. LOVEIT.

I do not, and I will have you think so!—What made you 180
hale me to this odious place, Bellinda?

BELLINDA.

I hate to be hulched up in a coach. Walking is much better.

MRS. LOVEIT.

Would we could meet Sir Fopling now!

BELLINDA.

Lord, would you not avoid him?

MRS. LOVEIT.

I would make him all the advances that may be.   185

BELLINDA.

That would confirm Dorimant's suspicion, my dear.

MRS. LOVEIT.

He is not jealous; but I will make him so, and be revenged
a way he little thinks on.

BELLINDA (aside).

If she should make him jealous, that may make him fond of
her again. I must dissuade her from it. —Lord, my dear, 190
this will certainly make him hate you.

MRS. LOVEIT.

'Twill make him uneasy, though he does not care for me. I
know the effects of jealousy on men of his proud temper.

BELLINDA.

'Tis a fantastic remedy: its operations are dangerous and
uncertain.   195

174. spoke] *Q1, 1704;* spoken *Q2-3.*

---

182. *hulched up*] hunched up.

MRS. LOVEIT.

'Tis the strongest cordial we can give to dying love. It often brings it back when there's no sign of life remaining. But I design not so much the reviving his, as my revenge.

Enter Sir Fopling *and his equipage.*

SIR FOPLING.

Hey! Bid the coachman send home four of his horses and bring the coach to Whitehall. I'll walk over the Park. [*To* 200 Mrs. Loveit.] Madam, the honor of kissing your fair hands is a happiness I missed this afternoon at my Lady Townley's.

MRS. LOVEIT.

You were very obliging, Sir Fopling, the last time I saw you there.

SIR FOPLING.

The preference was due to your wit and beauty. [*To* 205 Bellinda.] Madam, your servant. There never was so sweet an evening.

BELLINDA.

'T has drawn all the rabble of the town hither.

SIR FOPLING.

'Tis pity there's not an order made that none but the *beau monde* should walk here.   210

MRS. LOVEIT.

'Twould add much to the beauty of the place. See what a sort of nasty fellows are coming!

Enter four ill-fashioned fellows singing:

" 'Tis not for kisses alone, etc."

208. of] *Q 1–2, 1704;* in *Q 3.*

_____

200. *Whitehall*] royal palace, across the park from the Mall; destroyed by fire in 1698.

212.1. *four*] probably an error; "three slovenly bullies" are listed in the *dramatis personae*, and only three have speaking parts.

213. *'Tis . . . etc.*] ll. 5–8 of an anonymous song, "Tell me no more you love," published in *A New Collection of the Choicest Songs* (1676); and in *The Last and Best Edition of New Songs* (1677). The lines read: " 'Tis not for kisses alone/ So long I have made my address./ There's something else to be done,/ Which you cannot choose but guess." The song became the basis for a ballad, "Love al-a-Mode, or, the Modish Mistris" (Pepys Collection, III, 102; Pepysian Library, Magdalene College, Cambridge).

MRS. LOVEIT.

Foh! Their periwigs are scented with tobacco so strong—

SIR FOPLING.

—It overcomes our pulvilio. Methinks I smell the coffee- 215
house they come from.

FIRST MAN.

Dorimant's convenient, Madam Loveit.

SECOND MAN.

I like the oily buttock with her.

THIRD MAN [*pointing to* Sir Fopling].

What spruce prig is that?

FIRST MAN.

A caravan, lately come from Paris.   220

SECOND MAN.

Peace, they smoke!   *All of them coughing; exeunt singing:*
"There's something else to be done, etc."

Enter Dorimant *and* Medley.

DORIMANT.

They're engaged.

MEDLEY.

She entertains him as if she liked him.

DORIMANT.

Let us go forward, seem earnest in discourse, and show our- 225
selves. Then you shall see how she'll use him.

BELLINDA.

Yonder's Dorimant, my dear.

MRS. LOVEIT.

I see him. (*Aside.*) He comes insulting, but I will disappoint him in his expectation. (*To* Sir Fopling.) I like
this pretty, nice humor of yours, Sir Fopling. [*To* Bellinda.] 230
With what a loathing eye he looked upon those fellows!

SIR FOPLING.

I sat near one of 'em at a play today and was almost
poisoned with a pair of cordovan gloves he wears.

216. come] *Q 1–3;* came *1704.*

---

216. *pulvilio*] scented powder.   217. *convenient*] mistress.
218. *oily buttock*] smooth whore.   219. *spruce prig*] fop.
220. *caravan*] i.e., object for plunder.   221. *smoke*] notice (us).
222. *There's . . . etc.*] See note to l. 213, above.
233. *cordovan gloves*] gloves of cordovan leather, made of horsehide.

MRS. LOVEIT.

Oh, filthy cordovan! How I hate the smell!

Laughs in a loud, affected way.

SIR FOPLING.

Did you observe, madam, how their cravats hung loose an 235
inch from their neck, and what a frightful air it gave 'em?

MRS. LOVEIT.

Oh! I took particular notice of one that is always spruced
up with a deal of dirty, sky-colored ribbon.

BELLINDA.

That's one of the walking flageolets who haunt the Mail o'
nights.   240

MRS. LOVEIT.

Oh, I remember him. H' has a hollow tooth, enough to
spoil the sweetness of an evening.

SIR FOPLING.

I have seen the tallest walk the streets with a dainty pair of
boxes, neatly buckled on.

MRS. LOVEIT.

And a little footboy at his heels, pocket-high, with a flat cap, 245
a dirty face—

SIR FOPLING.

—And a snotty nose.

MRS. LOVEIT.

Oh, odious! There's many of my own sex, with that Holborn
equipage, trig to Gray's Inn Walks, and now and then
travel hither on a Sunday.   250

241. H' has] *Q1–3, 1704;* He's   249. trig] *Q1–3, 1704;* trip *Verity.*
Verity, Brett-Smith.

239. *flageolets*] flute-like instruments; hence, perhaps, tall, thin persons.
In colloquial French, *flûte* sometimes carries connotations of length and
thinness.
241. *H' has ... tooth*] See textual note. For his reading, Brett-Smith
cites Sparkish to Lucy in Wycherley, *The Country Wife*, Act V: "eternal
rotten-tooth."
244. *boxes*] wooden overshoes (?).
248-249. *Holborn equipage*] retinue characteristic of the middle class;
Holborn was a center of professional and commercial activity.
249. *trig*] walk briskly, trip.
249. *Gray's Inn Walks*] gardens of Gray's Inn, one of two Inns of Court
in Holborn.

MEDLEY [*to* Dorimant].

She takes no notice of you.

DORIMANT.

Damn her! I am jealous of a counterplot.

MRS. LOVEIT.

Your liveries are the finest, Sir Fopling. Oh, that page! That page is the prettily'st dressed. They are all French-men? 255

SIR FOPLING.

There's one damned English blockhead among 'em. You may know him by his mien.

MRS. LOVEIT.

Oh, that's he, that's he! What do you call him?

SIR FOPLING [*calling* Footman].

Hey!—I know not what to call him.

MRS. LOVEIT.

What's your name? 260

FOOTMAN.

John Trott, madam.

SIR FOPLING.

Oh, insufferable! Trott, Trott, Trott! There's nothing so barbarous as the names of our English servants. What countryman are you, sirrah?

FOOTMAN.

Hampshire, sir. 265

SIR FOPLING.

Then Hampshire be your name. Hey, Hampshire!

MRS. LOVEIT.

Oh, that sound! That sound becomes the mouth of a man of quality.

MEDLEY.

Dorimant, you look a little bashful on the matter.

DORIMANT.

She dissembles better than I thought she could have done. 270

MEDLEY.

You have tempted her with too luscious a bait. She bites at the coxcomb.

263–264. *What countryman are you*] i.e., What district are you from?

DORIMANT.

She cannot fall from loving me to that?

MEDLEY.

You begin to be jealous in earnest.

DORIMANT.

Of one I do not love?   275

MEDLEY.

You did love her.

DORIMANT.

The fit has long been over.

MEDLEY.

But I have known men fall into dangerous relapses when
they have found a woman inclining to another.

DORIMANT (*to himself*).

He guesses the secret of my heart. I am concerned but dare   280
not show it, lest Bellinda should mistrust all I have done to
gain her.

BELLINDA (*aside*).

I have watched his look and find no alteration there. Did he
love her, some signs of jealousy would have appeared.

DORIMANT [*to* Mrs. Loveit].

I hope this happy evening, madam, has reconciled you to   285
the scandalous Mail. We shall have you now hankering here
again.

MRS. LOVEIT.

Sir Fopling, will you walk?

SIR FOPLING.

I am all obedience, madam.

MRS. LOVEIT.

Come along then, and let's agree to be malicious on all the 290
ill-fashioned things we meet.

SIR FOPLING.

We'll make a critique on the whole Mail, madam.

MRS. LOVEIT.

Bellinda, you shall engage.

---

286. *hankering*] "hanging around" (expectantly).
293. *engage*] take part.

BELLINDA.

To the reserve of our friends, my dear.

MRS. LOVEIT.

No! No exceptions.   295

SIR FOPLING.

We'll sacrifice all to our diversion.

MRS. LOVEIT.

All, all.

SIR FOPLING.

All!

BELLINDA.

All? Then let it be.

       Exeunt Sir Fopling, Mrs. Loveit, Bellinda, *and* Pert, *laughing.*

MEDLEY.

Would you had brought some more of your friends, Dori- 300
mant, to have been witnesses of Sir Fopling's disgrace and
your triumph!

DORIMANT.

'Twere unreasonable to desire you not to laugh at me; but
pray do not expose me to the town this day or two.

MEDLEY.

By that time you hope to have regained your credit?   305

DORIMANT.

I know she hates Fopling and only makes use of him in hope
to work me on again. Had it not been for some powerful
considerations which will be removed tomorrow morning, I
had made her pluck off this mask and show the passion that
lies panting under.   310

                Enter a Footman.

MEDLEY.

Here comes a man from Bellair, with news of your last
adventure.

DORIMANT.

I am glad he sent him. I long to know the consequence of
our parting.

FOOTMAN.

Sir, my master desires you to come to my Lady Townley's 315

---

294. *To . . . of*] except for.

presently and bring Mr. Medley with you. My Lady
Woodvill and her daughter are there.

MEDLEY.

Then all's well, Dorimant.

FOOTMAN.

They have sent for the fiddles and mean to dance. He bid
me tell you, sir, the old lady does not know you; and would 320
have you own yourself to be Mr. Courtage. They are all
prepared to receive you by that name.

DORIMANT.

That foppish admirer of quality, who flatters the very meat
at honorable tables and never offers love to a woman below
a lady-grandmother!   325

MEDLEY.

You know the character you are to act, I see.

DORIMANT.

This is Harriet's contrivance—wild, witty, lovesome,
beautiful and young. —Come along, Medley.

MEDLEY.

This new woman would well supply the loss of Loveit.

DORIMANT.

That business must not end so. Before tomorrow sun is set, 330
I will revenge and clear it.

   And you and Loveit, to her cost, shall find
   I fathom all the depths of womankind.   *Exeunt.*

---

316. *presently*] immediately.
327–328. *wild . . . young*] Brett-Smith compares to Waller, "Of the
Danger his Majesty (Being Prince) Escaped in the Road at Saint Andrews,"
ll. 13–14: "Of the Fourth Edward was his noble song,/ Fierce, goodly,
valiant, beautiful, and young" (Thorn Drury, I, 1).

Act IV

[IV.i]

[*Lady Townley's.*] *The scene opens with the fiddles playing a country dance.
Enter* Dorimant [*and*] Lady Woodvill, Young Bellair *and* Mrs.
Harriet, Old Bellair *and* Emilia, Mr. Medley *and* Lady Townley, *as
having just ended the dance.*

OLD BELLAIR.

So, so, so! A smart bout, a very smart bout, adod!

LADY TOWNLEY.

How do you like Emilia's dancing, brother?

OLD BELLAIR.

Not at all, not at all!

LADY TOWNLEY.

You speak not what you think, I am sure.

OLD BELLAIR.

No matter for that; go, bid her dance no more. It don't   5
become her, it don't become her. Tell her I say so.
(*Aside.*)   Adod, I love her.

DORIMANT (*to* Lady Woodvill).

All people mingle nowadays, madam. And in public places
women of quality have the least respect showed 'em.

LADY WOODVILL.

I protest you say the truth, Mr. Courtage.   10

DORIMANT.

Forms and ceremonies, the only things that uphold quality
and greatness, are now shamefully laid aside and neglected.

LADY WOODVILL.

Well, this is not the women's age, let 'em think what they
will. Lewdness is the business now; love was the bus'ness in
my time.   15

DORIMANT.

The women, indeed, are little beholding to the young men
of this age. They're generally only dull admirers of themselves and make their court to nothing but their periwigs
and their cravats—and would be more concerned for the
disordering of 'em, though on a good occasion, than a young   20

16. beholding] *Q 1–2, 1704;* be-
holden *Q 3.*

maid would be for the tumbling of her head or handkercher.

LADY WOODVILL.

I protest you hit 'em.

DORIMANT.

They are very assiduous to show themselves at court, well-
dressed, to the women of quality; but their bus'ness is with
the stale mistresses of the town, who are prepared to receive   25
their lazy addresses by industrious old lovers who have cast
'em off and made 'em easy.

HARRIET [*to* Medley].

He fits my mother's humor so well, a little more and she'll
dance a kissing dance with him anon.

MEDLEY.

Dutifully observed, madam.   30

DORIMANT.

They pretend to be great critics in beauty—by their talk
you would think they liked no face—and yet can dote on an
ill one if it belong to a laundress or a tailor's daughter. They
cry a woman's past her prime at twenty, decayed at four-
and-twenty, old and insufferable at thirty.   35

LADY WOODVILL.

Insufferable at thirty! That they are in the wrong, Mr.
Courtage, at five-and-thirty there are living proofs enough
to convince 'em.

DORIMANT.

Ay, madam; there's Mrs. Setlooks, Mrs. Droplip, and my
Lady Loud. Show me among all our opening buds a face   40
that promises so much beauty as the remains of theirs.

LADY WOODVILL.

The depraved appetite of this vicious age tastes nothing but
green fruit and loathes it when 'tis kindly ripened.

DORIMANT.

Else so many deserving women, madam, would not be so
untimely neglected.   45

LADY WOODVILL.

I protest, Mr. Courtage, a dozen such good men as you

21. handkercher] *Q1–3;* handker-   26. have] *Q1–2, 1704; Q3 omits.*
chief *1704.*   35. old] *Q1–2, 1704; Q3 omits.*

21. *handkercher*] i.e., breast- or neck-handkerchief.
43. *kindly*] seasonably.

would be enough to atone for that wicked Dorimant and all
the under-debauchees of the town.

*Harriet, Emilia, Young Bellair, Medley, and Lady Townley break out
into a laughter.*

What's the matter there?

MEDLEY.

A pleasant mistake, madam, that a lady has made occasions   50
a little laughter.

OLD BELLAIR [*to* Dorimant *and* Lady Woodvill].

Come, come, you keep 'em idle! They are impatient till the
fiddles play again.

DORIMANT.

You are not weary, madam?

LADY WOODVILL.

One dance more. I cannot refuse you, Mr. Courtage.   55

They dance. After the dance, Old Bellair *singing and dancing up to* Emilia.

EMILIA.

You are very active, sir.

OLD BELLAIR.

Adod, sirrah, when I was a young fellow, I could ha'
capered up to my woman's gorget.

DORIMANT [*to* Lady Woodvill].

You are willing to rest yourself, madam?

LADY TOWNLEY [*to* Dorimant *and* Lady Woodvill].

We'll walk into my chamber and sit down.   60

MEDLEY.

Leave us Mr. Courtage; he's a dancer, and the young ladies
are not weary yet.

LADY WOODVILL.

We'll send him out again.

HARRIET.

If you do not quickly, I know where to send for Mr.
Dorimant.   65

LADY WOODVILL.

This girl's head, Mr. Courtage, is ever running on that wild
fellow.

59. yourself] *Q 1–3;* you self *1704.*

---

58. *capered . . . gorget*] kicked as high as my partner's neckpiece.

DORIMANT.

'Tis well you have got her a good husband, madam. That will settle it.

Exeunt Lady Townley, Lady Woodvill, *and* Dorimant.

OLD BELLAIR (*to* Emilia).

Adod, sweetheart, be advised and do not throw thyself   70
away on a young idle fellow.

EMILIA.

I have no such intention, sir.

OLD BELLAIR.

Have a little patience! Thou shalt have the man I spake of.
Adod, he loves thee and will make a good husband. But no
words—   75

EMILIA.

But, sir—

OLD BELLAIR.

No answer, out a pize! Peace, and think on't.

Enter Dorimant.

DORIMANT.

Your company is desired within, sir.

OLD BELLAIR.

I go, I go! Good Mr. Courtage, fare you well. (*To*
Emilia.)   Go, I'll see you no more!   80

EMILIA.

What have I done, sir?

OLD BELLAIR.

You are ugly, you are ugly!—Is she not, Mr. Courtage?

EMILIA.

Better words, or I shan't abide you!

OLD BELLAIR.

Out a pize! Adod, what does she say?—Hit her a pat for
me there.   *Exit* Old Bellair.   85

MEDLEY [*to* Dorimant].

You have charms for the whole family.

DORIMANT.

You'll spoil all with some unseasonable jest, Medley.

MEDLEY.

You see I confine my tongue and am content to be a bare
spectator, much contrary to my nature.

68. got] *Q1–2, 1704;* gotten *Q3.*   71. on] *Q1–2, 1704;* upon *Q3.*

EMILIA.

Methinks, Mr. Dorimant, my Lady Woodvill is a little fond   90
of you.

DORIMANT.

Would her daughter were.

MEDLEY.

It may be you may find her so. Try her. You have an
opportunity.

DORIMANT.

And I will not lose it. —Bellair, here's a lady has something   95
to say to you.

YOUNG BELLAIR.

I wait upon her. —Mr. Medley, we have both business with
you.

DORIMANT.

Get you all together, then.

[*He bows to* Harriet; *she curtsies.*]

(*To* Harriet.)   That demure curtsy is not amiss in jest, but   100
do not think in earnest it becomes you.

HARRIET.

Affectation is catching, I find. From your grave bow I got
it.

DORIMANT.

Where had you all that scorn and coldness in your look?

HARRIET.

From nature, sir; pardon my want of art. I have not learnt   105
those softnesses and languishings which now in faces are so
much in fashion.

DORIMANT.

You need 'em not. You have a sweetness of your own, if you
would but calm your frowns and let it settle.

HARRIET.

My eyes are wild and wand'ring like my passions, and can-   110
not yet be tied to rules of charming.

DORIMANT.

Women, indeed, have commonly a method of managing
those messengers of love. Now they will look as if they

113. will] *Q1–2, 1704; Q3 omits.*

would kill, and anon they will look as if they were dying.
They point and rebate their glances, the better to invite us. 115

HARRIET.

I like this variety well enough, but hate the set face that
always looks as it would say, "Come love me"—a woman
who at plays makes the *doux yeux* to a whole audience and at
home cannot forbear 'em to her monkey.

DORIMANT.

Put on a gentle smile and let me see how well it will become 120
you.

HARRIET.

I am sorry my face does not please you as it is; but I shall
not be complaisant and change it.

DORIMANT.

Though you are obstinate, I know 'tis capable of improve-
ment, and shall do you justice, madam, if I chance to be at 125
court when the critics of the circle pass their judgment; for
thither you must come.

HARRIET.

And expect to be taken in pieces, have all my features
examined, every motion censured, and on the whole be
condemned to be but pretty—or a beauty of the lowest rate. 130
What think you?

DORIMANT.

The women—nay, the very lovers who belong to the drawing room—will maliciously allow you more than that. They
always grant what is apparent, that they may the better be
believed when they name concealed faults they cannot 135
easily be disproved in.

HARRIET.

Beauty runs as great a risk exposed at court as wit does on the
stage, where the ugly and the foolish all are free to censure.

DORIMANT (*aside*).

I love her and dare not let her know it. I fear sh'as an

---

115. *point and rebate*] sharpen and blunt.
118. *makes . . . to*] "makes eyes at."
126. *the circle*] the assembly at court.
132–133. *drawing room*] where court receptions took place; *drawing room*
came to mean the assembly itself.

ascendant o'er me and may revenge the wrongs I have done 140
her sex. (*To her.*) Think of making a party, madam;
love will engage.

HARRIET.

You make me start. I did not think to have heard of love
from you.

DORIMANT.

I never knew what 'twas to have a settled ague yet, but now 145
and then have had irregular fits.

HARRIET.

Take heed; sickness after long health is commonly more
violent and dangerous.

DORIMANT (*aside*).

I have took the infection from her and feel the disease now
spreading in me. (*To her.*) Is the name of love so frightful 150
that you dare not stand it?

HARRIET.

'Twill do little execution out of your mouth on me, I am
sure.

DORIMANT.

It has been fatal—

HARRIET.

To some easy women, but we are not all born to one destiny. 155
I was informed you use to laugh at love, and not make it.

DORIMANT.

The time has been, but now I must speak.

HARRIET.

If it be on that idle subject, I will put on my serious look,
turn my head carelessly from you, drop my lip, let my eyelids
fall and hang half o'er my eyes—thus, while you buzz a 160
speech of an hour long in my ear and I answer never a word.
Why do you not begin?

DORIMANT.

That the company may take notice how passionately I
made advances of love and how disdainfully you receive
'em.   165

---

140. *ascendant*] domination; originally, an astrological term.
141. *making a party*] "entering the lists."
145. *ague*] fever.

HARRIET.

When your love's grown strong enough to make you bear being laughed at, I'll give you leave to trouble me with it. Till when, pray forbear, sir.

Enter Sir Fopling *and others in masks.*

DORIMANT.

What's here—masquerades?

HARRIET.

I thought that foppery had been left off, and people might 170 have been in private with a fiddle.

DORIMANT.

'Tis endeavored to be kept on foot still by some who find themselves the more acceptable, the less they are known.

YOUNG BELLAIR.

This must be Sir Fopling.

MEDLEY.

That extraordinary habit shows it.   175

YOUNG BELLAIR.

What are the rest?

MEDLEY.

A company of French rascals whom he picked up in Paris and has brought over to be his dancing equipage on these occasions. Make him own himself; a fool is very troublesome when he presumes he is incognito.   180

SIR FOPLING (*to* Harriet).

Do you know me?

HARRIET.

Ten to one but I guess at you.

SIR FOPLING.

Are you women as fond of a vizard as we men are?

HARRIET.

I am very fond of a vizard that covers a face I do not like, sir.   185

YOUNG BELLAIR.

Here are no masks, you see, sir, but those which came with

166. enough] *Q 1-2, 1704; Q 3 omits.*

---

175. *habit*] attire.

you. This was intended a private meeting; but because you look like a gentleman, if you will discover yourself and we know you to be such, you shall be welcome.

SIR FOPLING (*pulling off his mask*).

Dear Bellair.   190

MEDLEY.

Sir Fopling! How came you hither?

SIR FOPLING.

Faith, as I was coming late from Whitehall, after the King's *couchée*, one of my people told me he had heard fiddles at my Lady Townley's, and—

DORIMANT.

You need not say any more, sir.   195

SIR FOPLING.

Dorimant, let me kiss thee.

DORIMANT.

Hark you, Sir Fopling—   *Whispers.*

SIR FOPLING.

Enough, enough, Courtage. —[*Glancing at* Harriet.]   A pretty kind of young woman that, Medley. I observed her in the Mail, more *éveillée* than our English women commonly 200 are. Prithee, what is she?

MEDLEY.

The most noted *coquette* in town. Beware of her.

SIR FOPLING.

Let her be what she will, I know how to take my measures. In Paris the mode is to flatter the *prude*, laugh at the *faux-prude*, make serious love to the *demi-prude*, and only rally with 205 the *coquette*. Medley, what think you?

MEDLEY.

That for all this smattering of the mathematics, you may be out in your judgment at tennis.

188. will] *Q 1–3; 1704 omits.*   203. take] *Q 1, 1704;* make *Q 2–3.*
190. S.D. off] *Q 3, 1704; of Q 1–2.*   205. with] *Q 1, 1704;* at *Q 2–3.*
192. as] *Q 1–3; 1704 omits.*

193. *couchée*] evening reception.
200. *éveillée*] sprightly.
203. *to . . . measures*] to set my plans; an idiom from the French (*prendre des mesures*), of which the *OED* cites no English use before 1698.
204–205. *faux-prude*] false prude.
205. *demi-prude*] would-be prude.

SIR FOPLING.

What a *coq-à-l'âne* is this? I talk of women, and thou
answer'st tennis. 210

MEDLEY.

Mistakes will be, for want of apprehension.

SIR FOPLING.

I am very glad of the acquaintance I have with this family.

MEDLEY.

My lady truly is a good woman.

SIR FOPLING.

Ah, Dorimant—Courtage, I would say—would thou hadst
spent the last winter in Paris with me. When thou wert 215
there, La Corneus and Sallyes were the only habitudes we
had; a comedian would have been a *bonne fortune*. No
stranger ever passed his time so well as I did some months
before I came over. I was well received in a dozen families,
where all the women of quality used to visit. I have intrigues 220
to tell thee more pleasant than ever thou read'st in a novel.

HARRIET.

Write 'em, sir, and oblige us women. Our language wants
such little stories.

SIR FOPLING.

Writing, madam, 's a mechanic part of wit. A gentleman
should never go beyond a song or a *billet*. 225

HARRIET.

Bussy was a gentleman.

SIR FOPLING.

Who, d'Ambois?

220. to visit] *Q1, 1704;* to come to   224. madam, 's] *Q1–3;* madam, is
visit *Q2–3.*   *1704.*

---

209. *coq-à-l'âne*] string of nonsense.

216. *La Corneus and Sallyes*] Verity suggests Mesdames Cornuel and
Selles, minor literary figures of the day.

216. *habitudes*] i.e., acquaintances; Sir Fopling thinks of the French
idiom, *avoir ses habitudes dans une maison*, to be at home in someone's
house.

217. *a comedian . . . fortune*] The implication is that *even* a comic
actor would have been a "piece of good luck." Probably Sir Fopling shows
his ignorance; Madame Cornuel was known for her wit.

226. *Bussy*] Roger de Rabutin, Comte de Bussy (1618–1693); author of
the *Histoire Amoureuse des Gaules.*

227. *d'Ambois*] sixteenth-century French adventurer, who, as Bussy
d'Ambois, was titular hero of a play by George Chapman; by now, Sir
Fopling's ignorance is unmistakable.

MEDLEY [aside].

Was there ever such a brisk blockhead?

HARRIET.

Not d'Ambois, sir, but Rabutin: he who writ the *Loves of
France*.   230

SIR FOPLING.

That may be, madam; many gentlemen do things that are
below 'em. —Damn your authors, Courtage. Women are
the prettiest things we can fool away our time with.

HARRIET.

I hope ye have wearied yourself tonight at court, sir, and
will not think of fooling with anybody here.   235

SIR FOPLING.

I cannot complain of my fortune there, madam.—
Dorimant—

DORIMANT.

Again!

SIR FOPLING.

Courtage, a pox on't! I have something to tell thee. When I
had made my court within, I came out and flung myself 240
upon the mat under the state i' th' outward room, i' th'
midst of half a dozen beauties who were withdrawn to jeer
among themselves, as they called it.

DORIMANT.

Did you know 'em?

SIR FOPLING.

Not one of 'em, by heav'ns, not I! But they were all your 245
friends.

DORIMANT.

How are you sure of that?

SIR FOPLING.

Why, we laughed at all the town—spared nobody but yourself. They found me a man for their purpose.

234. ye] *Q1, 1704;* you *Q2–3.*   242. jeer] jeèr *Q1–2, 1704;* jeér *Q3.*
235. will] *Q1, 1704;* I will *Q2–3.*

---

241. *state*] canopy.
242. *jeer*] See textual note; apparently Sir Fopling gives the word a
pseudo-French accent.

DORIMANT.

I know you are malicious to your power.   250

SIR FOPLING.

And, faith, I had occasion to show it; for I never saw more
gaping fools at a ball or on a birthday.

DORIMANT.

You learned who the women were?

SIR FOPLING.

No matter; they frequent the drawing room.

DORIMANT.

And entertain themselves at the expense of all the fops who 255
come there.

SIR FOPLING.

That's their bus'ness. Faith, I sifted 'em and find they have
a sort of wit among them.

Pinches a tallow candle.

Ah, filthy!

DORIMANT.

Look, he has been pinching the tallow candle.   260

SIR FOPLING.

How can you breathe in a room where there's grease
frying? Dorimant, thou art intimate with my lady: advise
her, for her own sake and the good company that comes
hither, to burn wax lights.

HARRIET.

What are these masquerades who stand so obsequiously at a 265
distance?

SIR FOPLING.

A set of balladines, whom I picked out of the best in France
and brought over with a *flûte douce* or two—my servants.
They shall entertain you.

HARRIET.

I had rather see you dance yourself, Sir Fopling.   270

SIR FOPLING.

And I had rather do it—all the company knows it. But,
madam—

---

250. *to your power*] to the extent of your power.
252. *birthday*] celebration of the King's birthday.
257. *sifted 'em*] questioned them, got to know them.

MEDLEY.

Come, come, no excuses, Sir Fopling!

SIR FOPLING.

By heav'ns, Medley—

MEDLEY.

Like a woman I find you must be struggled with before one 275
brings you to what you desire.

HARRIET (aside).

Can he dance?

EMILIA.

And fence and sing too, if you'll believe him.

DORIMANT.

He has no more excellence in his heels than in his head. He
went to Paris a plain, bashful English blockhead and is 280
returned a fine, undertaking French fop.

MEDLEY [to Harriet].

I cannot prevail.

SIR FOPLING.

Do not think it want of complaisance, madam.

HARRIET.

You are too well-bred to want that, Sir Fopling. I think it
want of power.   285

SIR FOPLING.

By heav'ns, and so it is! I have sat up so damned late and
drunk so cursed hard since I came to this lewd town that I
am fit for nothing but low dancing now—a *courante*, a
bourrée, or a *menuet*. But St. André tells me, if I will but be
regular, in one month I shall rise again.   290

Endeavors at a caper.

Pox on this debauchery!

EMILIA.

I have heard your dancing much commended.

274. Medley] *Q 1, 1704; Q 2-3*   276. to] *1704; Q 1-3 omit.*
omit.   286. sat] *Q 1-2, 1704; sate Q 3.*

---

281. *undertaking*] bold.
288–289. *a courante . . . menuet*] *low* dances because they required no
capers.
289. *St. André*] French dancing-master, active on the English stage.

SIR FOPLING.

It had the good fortune to please in Paris. I was judged to
rise within an inch as high as the Basque in an entry I
danced there.   295

HARRIET [*to* Emilia].

I am mightily taken with this fool. Let us sit. —Here's a
seat, Sir Fopling.

SIR FOPLING.

At your feet, madam. I can be nowhere so much at ease.
—By your leave, gown.   [*Sits.*]

HARRIET. EMILIA.

Ah, you'll spoil it!   300

SIR FOPLING.

ı No matter, my clothes are my creatures. I make 'em to make
my court to you ladies. —Hey, *qu'on commence*!

Dance.

To an English dancer, English motions! I was forced to
entertain this fellow [*pointing to John Trott*], one of my set
miscarrying. —Oh, horrid! Leave your damned manner of 305
dancing and put on the French air. Have you not a pattern
before you?—Pretty well! Imitation in time may bring him
to something.

After the dance, enter Old Bellair, Lady Woodvill, *and* Lady Townley.

OLD BELLAIR.

Hey, adod, what have we here? A mumming?

LADY WOODVILL.

Where's my daughter?—Harriet!   310

DORIMANT.

Here, here, madam. I know not but under these disguises
there may be dangerous sparks. I gave the lady warning.

293. good] *Q 1, 1704; Q 2–3 omit.*
_____

294. *the Basque*] a Basque dancer of the age (?); otherwise, *basque,* the
skirt of a doublet.

294. *entry*] dance performed as interlude to an entertainment.

302. *qu'on commence*] begin!   304. *entertain*] hire.

305. *miscarrying*] Various senses are possible: coming to harm, leaving
my service, etc.

309. *mumming*] Mummers' plays were elaborately costumed folk drama.

LADY WOODVILL.

Lord, I am so obliged to you, Mr. Courtage.

HARRIET.

Lord, how you admire this man!

LADY WOODVILL.

What have you to except against him?   315

HARRIET.

He's a fop.

LADY WOODVILL.

He's not a Dorimant, a wild, extravagant fellow of the times.

HARRIET.

He's a man made up of forms and commonplaces, sucked
out of the remaining lees of the last age.

LADY WOODVILL.

He's so good a man that were you not engaged—   320

LADY TOWNLEY.

You'll have but little night to sleep in.

LADY WOODVILL.

Lord, 'tis perfect day!

DORIMANT (*aside*).

The hour is almost come I appointed Bellinda, and I am
not so foppishly in love here to forget. I am flesh and blood
yet.   325

LADY TOWNLEY.

I am very sensible, madam.

LADY WOODVILL.

Lord, madam—

HARRIET.

Look, in what a struggle is my poor mother yonder!

YOUNG BELLAIR.

She has much ado to bring out the compliment.

DORIMANT.

She strains hard for it.   330

HARRIET.

See, see—her head tottering, her eyes staring, and her
underlip trembling.

328. a] *Q 1–3; 1704 omits.*

---

322. *perfect day*] broad daylight; see l. 413, below.
326. *sensible*] grateful, conscious of (your courtesy).

DORIMANT.

Now, now she's in the very convulsions of her civility. (*Aside.*) 'Sdeath, I shall lose Bellinda! I must fright her hence. She'll be an hour in this fit of good manners else. 335 (*To* Lady Woodvill.) Do you not know Sir Fopling, madam?

LADY WOODVILL.

I have seen that face. Oh heav'n, 'tis the same we met in the Mail! How came he here?

DORIMANT.

A fiddle in this town is a kind of fop-call. No sooner it 340 strikes up, but the house is besieged with an army of masquerades straight.

LADY WOODVILL.

Lord, I tremble, Mr. Courtage. For certain Dorimant is in the company.

DORIMANT.

I cannot confidently say he is not. You had best begone; I 345 will wait upon you. Your daughter is in the hands of Mr. Bellair.

LADY WOODVILL.

I'll see her before me. —Harriet, come away!

[*Exeunt* Lady Woodvill *and* Harriet.]

YOUNG BELLAIR.

Lights, lights!

LADY TOWNLEY.

Light, down there! 350

OLD BELLAIR.

Adod, it needs not—

[*Exeunt* Lady Townley *and* Young Bellair.]

DORIMANT [*calling to the servants outside*].

Call my Lady Woodvill's coach to the door! Quickly!

[*Exit* Dorimant.]

OLD BELLAIR.

Stay, Mr. Medley; let the young fellows do that duty. We will drink a glass of wine together. 'Tis good after dancing. [*Looks at* Sir Fopling.] What mumming spark is that? 355

MEDLEY.

He is not to be comprehended in few words.

SIR FOPLING.

Hey, La Tour!

MEDLEY.

Whither away, Sir Fopling?

SIR FOPLING.

I have bus'ness with Courtage.

MEDLEY.

He'll but put the ladies into their coach and come up again. 360

OLD BELLAIR.

In the meantime I'll call for a bottle.   *Exit* Old Bellair.

Enter Young Bellair.

MEDLEY.

Where's Dorimant?

YOUNG BELLAIR.

Stol'n home. He has had business waiting for him there all
this night, I believe, by an impatience I observed in him.

MEDLEY.

Very likely. 'Tis but dissembling drunkenness, railing at his 365
friends, and the kind soul will embrace the blessing and
forget the tedious expectation.

SIR FOPLING.

I must speak with him before I sleep.

YOUNG BELLAIR [*to* Medley].

Emilia and I are resolved on that business.

MEDLEY.

Peace, here's your father.   370

Enter Old Bellair *and butler with a bottle of wine.*

OLD BELLAIR.

The women are all gone to bed. —Fill, boy!—Mr. Medley,
begin a health.

MEDLEY (*whispers*).

To Emilia.

OLD BELLAIR.

Out a pize! She's a rogue, and I'll not pledge you.

MEDLEY.

I know you will.   375

375. will] *CBEP, Verity, Brett-Smith;*
well *Q 1–3, 1704.*

OLD BELLAIR.

Adod, drink it, then!

SIR FOPLING.

Let us have the new bachique.

OLD BELLAIR.

Adod, that is a hard word! What does it mean, sir?

MEDLEY.

A catch or drinking song.

OLD BELLAIR.

Let us have it, then.   380

SIR FOPLING.

Fill the glasses round, and draw up in a body. —Hey,
music!

They sing.

The pleasures of love and the joys of good wine,
To perfect our happiness wisely we join.
We to beauty all day   385
Give the sovereign sway
And her favorite nymphs devoutly obey;
At the plays we are constantly making our court,
And when they are ended, we follow the sport
To the Mail and the Park,   390
Where we love till 'tis dark.
Then sparkling champagne
Puts an end to their reign:
It quickly recovers
Poor languishing lovers,   395
Makes us frolic and gay, and drowns all our sorrow;
But alas, we relapse again on the morrow.
    Let every man stand
    With his glass in his hand,

378. that is] *Q1, 1704;* that's *Q2-3.*   390. Mail] *Q2-3, 1704;* Mall *Q1.*

377. *bachique*] cited by the *OED* as a sole instance of *bacchic* in the
meaning of "drinking song"; cf. *chanson bachique* (Fr.).
   383-384. *The pleasures . . . join*] Cf. lines from two songs in Thomas
Shadwell's *Psyche* (1675), Act V: 1) "*The Delights of the Bottle, and the
Charms of Good Wine,/ To the power and the pleasures of Love must resign.*" 2)
"*Were it not for the Pleasures of Love and good Wine,/ Mankind for each trifle their
lives would resign*" (*The Complete Works of Thomas Shadwell*, ed. Montague
Summers [London, 1927], II, 338).

And briskly discharge at the word of command.   400
    Here's a health to all those
    Whom tonight we depose.
Wine and beauty by turns great souls should inspire;
Present all together; and now, boys, give fire!

                [*They drink.*]

OLD BELLAIR.

Adod, a pretty bus'ness and very merry!   405

SIR FOPLING.

Hark you, Medley, let you and I take the fiddles and go
waken Dorimant.

MEDLEY.

We shall do him a courtesy, if it be as I guess. For after the
fatigue of this night, he'll quickly have his belly full and be
glad of an occasion to cry, "Take away, Handy!"   410

YOUNG BELLAIR.

I'll go with you; and there we'll consult about affairs,
Medley.

OLD BELLAIR (*looks on his watch*).

Adod, 'tis six o'clock!

SIR FOPLING.

Let's away, then.

OLD BELLAIR.

Mr. Medley, my sister tells me you are an honest man. And,   415
adod, I love you. —Few words and hearty, that's the way
with old Harry, old Harry.

SIR FOPLING [*to his servants*].

Light your flambeaux! Hey!

OLD BELLAIR.

What does the man mean?

MEDLEY.

'Tis day, Sir Fopling.   420

SIR FOPLING.

No matter; our serenade will look the greater.   *Exeunt omnes.*

[IV.ii]

Dorimant's lodging; a table, a candle, a toilet, etc. Handy *tying up linen.*
Enter Dorimant *in his gown, and* Bellinda.

403. should] *Q1, 1704;* shall *Q2-3.*

418. *flambeaux*] torches.

DORIMANT.

Why will you be gone so soon?

BELLINDA.

Why did you stay out so late?

DORIMANT.

Call a chair, Handy.   [*Exit* Handy.]

—What makes you tremble so?

BELLINDA.

I have a thousand fears about me. Have I not been seen,   5
think you?

DORIMANT.

By nobody but myself and trusty Handy.

BELLINDA.

Where are all your people?

DORIMANT.

I have dispersed 'em on sleeveless errands. What does that
sigh mean?   10

BELLINDA.

Can you be so unkind to ask me? Well (*sighs*), were it to do
again—

DORIMANT.

We should do it, should we not?

BELLINDA.

I think we should: the wickeder man you, to make me love
so well. Will you be discreet now?   15

DORIMANT.

I will.

BELLINDA.

You cannot.

DORIMANT.

Never doubt it.

BELLINDA.

I will not expect it.

DORIMANT.

You do me wrong.   20

BELLINDA.

You have no more power to keep the secret than I had not
to trust you with it.

_____

9. *sleeveless*] useless.

DORIMANT.

By all the joys I have had and those you keep in store—

BELLINDA.

—You'll do for my sake what you never did before.

DORIMANT.

By that truth thou hast spoken, a wife shall sooner betray   25
herself to her husband.

BELLINDA.

Yet I had rather you should be false in this than in another
thing you promised me.

DORIMANT.

What's that?

BELLINDA.

That you would never see Loveit more but in public places   30
—in the Park, at court and plays.

DORIMANT.

'Tis not likely a man should be fond of seeing a damned old
play when there is a new one acted.

BELLINDA.

I dare not trust your promise.

DORIMANT.

You may.   35

BELLINDA.

This does not satisfy me. You shall swear you never will see
her more.

DORIMANT.

I will, a thousand oaths. By all—

BELLINDA.

Hold! You shall not, now I think on't better.

DORIMANT.

I will swear!   40

BELLINDA.

I shall grow jealous of the oath and think I owe your truth
to that, not to your love.

DORIMANT.

Then, by my love! No other oath I'll swear.

Enter Handy.

27. another] *Q 1–3;* any other *1704.*

HANDY.

Here's a chair.

BELLINDA.

Let me go.   45

DORIMANT.

I cannot.

BELLINDA.

Too willingly, I fear.

DORIMANT.

Too unkindly feared. When will you promise me again?

BELLINDA.

Not this fortnight.

DORIMANT.

You will be better than your word.   50

BELLINDA.

I think I shall. Will it not make you love me less?

Fiddles without.

(*Starting.*)   Hark, what fiddles are these?

DORIMANT.

Look out, Handy.   *Exit* Handy *and returns.*

HANDY.

Mr. Medley, Mr. Bellair, and Sir Fopling. They are
coming up.   55

DORIMANT.

How got they in?

HANDY.

The door was open for the chair.

BELLINDA.

Lord, let me fly!

DORIMANT.

Here, here, down the back stairs. I'll see you into your
chair.   60

BELLINDA.

No, no, stay and receive 'em. And be sure you keep your
word and never see Loveit more. Let it be a proof of your
kindness.

DORIMANT.

It shall. —Handy, direct her. —(*Kissing her hand.*)   Ever-
lasting love go along with thee.   65

Exeunt Bellinda and Handy.

Enter Young Bellair, Medley, *and* Sir Fopling [*with his page*].

YOUNG BELLAIR.

Not abed yet?

MEDLEY.

You have had an irregular fit, Dorimant.

DORIMANT.

I have.

YOUNG BELLAIR.

And is it off already?

DORIMANT.

Nature has done her part, gentlemen. When she falls kindly   70
to work, great cures are effected in little time, you know.

SIR FOPLING.

We thought there was a wench in the case, by the chair that
waited. Prithee, make us a *confidence*.

DORIMANT.

Excuse me.

SIR FOPLING.

Le sage Dorimant. Was she pretty?   75

DORIMANT.

So pretty she may come to keep her coach and pay parish
duties, if the good humor of the age continue.

MEDLEY.

And be of the number of the ladies kept by public-spirited
men for the good of the whole town.

SIR FOPLING.

Well said, Medley.   80

Sir Fopling *dancing by himself.*

YOUNG BELLAIR.

See Sir Fopling dancing.

DORIMANT.

You are practicing and have a mind to recover, I see.

SIR FOPLING.

Prithee, Dorimant, why hast not thou a glass hung up here?
A room is the dullest thing without one.

---

67. *irregular fit*] See IV.i.146; Medley has overheard Dorimant.
75. *Le sage*] prudent.

YOUNG BELLAIR.

Here is company to entertain you.   85

SIR FOPLING.

But I mean in case of being alone. In a glass a man may
entertain himself—

DORIMANT.

The shadow of himself, indeed.

SIR FOPLING.

—Correct the errors of his motions and his dress.

MEDLEY.

I find, Sir Fopling, in your solitude you remember the   90
saying of the wise man, and study yourself.

SIR FOPLING.

'Tis the best diversion in our retirements. Dorimant, thou
art a pretty fellow and wear'st thy clothes well, but I never
saw thee have a handsome cravat. Were they made up like
mine, they'd give another air to thy face. Prithee, let me   95
send my man to dress thee but one day. By heav'ns, an
Englishman cannot tie a ribbon!

DORIMANT.

They are something clumsy-fisted.

SIR FOPLING.

I have brought over the prettiest fellow that ever spread a
toilet. He served some time under Merille, the greatest genie   100
in the world for a *valet de chambre*.

DORIMANT.

What, he who formerly belonged to the Duke of Candale?

SIR FOPLING.

The same, and got him his immortal reputation.

DORIMANT.

Y' have a very fine brandenburgh on, Sir Fopling.

SIR FOPLING.

It serves to wrap me up, after the fatigue of a ball.   105

104. Y' have] *Q 1–3;* Y'ave *1704.*

---

100. *Merille*] valet to the Duke of Orleans, brother of Louis XIV.
100. *genie*] genius.
102. *Duke of Candale*] Louis-Charles-Gaston de Nogaret de Foix (1627–
1658); French general, who figures in Bussy's *Histoire Amoureuse des Gaules*.
104. *brandenburgh*] woolen morning gown.

MEDLEY.

I see you often in it, with your periwig tied up.

SIR FOPLING.

We should not always be in a set dress. 'Tis more *en cavalier*
to appear now and then in a *déshabillé*.

MEDLEY.

Pray, how goes your business with Loveit?

SIR FOPLING.

You might have answered yourself in the Mail last night.   110
—Dorimant, did you not see the advances she made me? I
have been endeavoring at a song.

DORIMANT.

Already?

SIR FOPLING.

'Tis my *coup d'essai* in English. I would fain have thy opinion
of it.   115

DORIMANT.

Let's see it.

SIR FOPLING.

Hey, page, give me my song. —Bellair, here. Thou hast a
pretty voice; sing it.

YOUNG BELLAIR.

Sing it yourself, Sir Fopling.

SIR FOPLING.

Excuse me.   120

YOUNG BELLAIR.

You learnt to sing in Paris.

SIR FOPLING.

I did—of Lambert, the greatest master in the world; but I
have his own fault, a weak voice, and care not to sing out of
a *ruelle*.

DORIMANT.

A *ruelle* is a pretty cage for a singing fop, indeed.   125

110. yourself] *Q 1–3; you self 1704.*

---

107. *en cavalier*] "dashing."   108. *in a déshabillé*] informally dressed.
114. *coup d'essai*] first attempt.
122. *Lambert*] Michel Lambert (1610–1696); singer, composer, and
master of chamber music to Louis XIV.
124. *ruelle*] lady's bedchamber, where morning receptions were sometimes held.

Young Bellair *reads the song.*

How charming Phillis is, how fair!
    Ah, that she were as willing
To ease my wounded heart of care,
    And make her eyes less killing.
I sigh, I sigh, I languish now,   130
    And love will not let me rest;
I drive about the Park and bow,
    Still as I meet my dearest.

SIR FOPLING.

Sing it, sing it, man! It goes to a pretty new tune which I
am confident was made by Baptiste.   135

MEDLEY.

Sing it yourself, Sir Fopling. He does not know the tune.

SIR FOPLING.

I'll venture.

                    Sir Fopling *sings.*

DORIMANT.

Ay, marry, now 'tis something. I shall not flatter you, Sir
Fopling: there is not much thought in't, but 'tis passionate
and well-turned.   140

MEDLEY.

After the French way.

SIR FOPLING.

That I aimed at. Does it not give you a lively image of the
thing? Slap, down goes the glass, and thus we are at it.

                    [*He bows and grimaces.*]

DORIMANT.

It does indeed. I perceive, Sir Fopling, you'll be the very
head of the sparks who are lucky in compositions of this 145
nature.

                    Enter Sir Fopling's Footman.

SIR FOPLING.

La Tour, is the bath ready?

139. 'tis] *Q1, Q3, 1704;* 'is *Q2.*

---

133. *Still as*] whenever.
135. *Baptiste*] Jean Baptiste Lully (1633–1687); composer, director of
opera, and master of court music to Louis XIV.
143. *glass*] i.e., coach window.

FOOTMAN.

Yes, sir.

SIR FOPLING.

Adieu donc, mes chers.

Exit Sir Fopling [*with his* Footman *and page*].

MEDLEY.

When have you your revenge on Loveit, Dorimant?   150

DORIMANT.

I will but change my linen and about it.

MEDLEY.

The powerful considerations which hindered have been removed, then?

DORIMANT.

Most luckily, this morning. You must along with me; my reputation lies at stake there.   155

MEDLEY.

I am engaged to Bellair.

DORIMANT.

What's your business?

MEDLEY.

Ma-tri-mony, an't like you.

DORIMANT.

It does not, sir.

YOUNG BELLAIR.

It may in time, Dorimant. What think you of Mrs. Harriet?   160

DORIMANT.

What does she think of me?

YOUNG BELLAIR.

I am confident she loves you.

DORIMANT.

How does it appear?

YOUNG BELLAIR.

Why, she's never well but when she's talking of you, but then she finds all the faults in you she can. She laughs at all who   165 commend you; but then she speaks ill of all who do not.

DORIMANT.

Women of her temper betray themselves by their over-

---

149. *Adieu . . . chers*] Farewell, dear fellows.
158. *an't*] if it (dial.).

cunning. I had once a growing love with a lady who would
always quarrel with me when I came to see her, and yet was
never quiet if I stayed a day from her.   170

YOUNG BELLAIR.

My father is in love with Emilia.

DORIMANT.

That is a good warrant for your proceedings. Go on and
prosper; I must to Loveit. —Medley, I am sorry you cannot
be a witness.

MEDLEY.

Make her meet Sir Fopling again in the same place and use 175
him ill before me.

DORIMANT.

That may be brought about, I think. —I'll be at your
aunt's anon and give you joy, Mr. Bellair.

YOUNG BELLAIR.

You had best not think of Mrs. Harriet too much. Without
church security, there's no taking up there.   180

DORIMANT.

I may fall into the snare, too. But,
    The wise will find a difference in our fate:
    You wed a woman, I a good estate.   *Exeunt.*

[IV.iii]

[*The Mail; in front of Mrs. Loveit's.*] *Enter the chair with* Bellinda; *the
men set it down and open it.* Bellinda *starting.*

BELLINDA (*surprised*).

Lord, where am I? In the Mail! Whither have you brought
me?

FIRST CHAIRMAN.

You gave us no directions, madam.

BELLINDA (*aside*).

The fright I was in made me forget it.

FIRST CHAIRMAN.

We use to carry a lady from the squire's hither.   5

---

178. *give you joy*] congratulate you.

180. *taking up*] In the metaphor established by "church security," *taking
up* means "borrowing (at interest)."

BELLINDA (*aside*).

    This is Loveit! I am undone if she sees me. —Quickly, carry
me away!

FIRST CHAIRMAN.

    Whither, an't like your honor?

BELLINDA.

    Ask no questions!

Enter Mrs. Loveit's Footman.

FOOTMAN.

    Have you seen my lady, madam?   10

BELLINDA.

    I am just come to wait upon her.

FOOTMAN.

    She will be glad to see you, madam. She sent me to you this
morning to desire your company, and I was told you went
out by five o'clock.

BELLINDA (*aside*).

    More and more unlucky!   15

FOOTMAN.

    Will you walk in, madam?

BELLINDA.

    I'll discharge my chair and follow. Tell your mistress I am
here.   *Exit* Footman.

[Bellinda] gives the Chairmen *money.*

    Take this; and if ever you should be examined, be sure you
say you took me up in the Strand, over against the Ex- 20
change—as you will answer it to Mr. Dorimant.

CHAIRMEN.

    We will, an't like your honor.   *Exeunt* Chairmen.

BELLINDA.

    Now to come off, I must on:

        In confidence and lies some hope is left;
        'Twere hard to be found out in the first theft.   25

                                Exit.

ACT V

[V.i]

[*Mrs. Loveit's.*] *Enter* Mrs. Loveit *and* Pert, *her woman.*

PERT.

Well! In my eyes, Sir Fopling is no such despicable person.

MRS. LOVEIT.

You are an excellent judge.

PERT.

He's as handsome a man as Mr. Dorimant, and as great a
gallant.

MRS. LOVEIT.

Intolerable! Is't not enough I submit to his impertinences,   5
but must I be plagued with yours too?

PERT.

Indeed, madam—

MRS. LOVEIT.

'Tis false, mercenary malice—

Enter her Footman.

FOOTMAN.

Mrs. Bellinda, madam.

MRS. LOVEIT.

What of her?   10

FOOTMAN.

She's below.

MRS. LOVEIT.

How came she?

FOOTMAN.

In a chair; ambling Harry brought her.

MRS. LOVEIT [*aside*].

He bring her! His chair stands near Dorimant's door and
always brings me from thence. —Run and ask him where he   15
took her up. Go!   [*Exit* Footman.]
There is no truth in friendship neither. Women as well as
men, all are false, or all are so to me at least.

PERT.

You are jealous of her too?

MRS. LOVEIT.

You had best tell her I am. 'Twill become the liberty you   20

take of late. [*Aside.*] This fellow's bringing of her, her
going out by five o'clock—I know not what to think.

Enter Bellinda.

Bellinda, you are grown an early riser, I hear.

BELLINDA.

Do you not wonder, my dear, what made me abroad so
soon?   25

MRS. LOVEIT.

You do not use to be so.

BELLINDA.

The country gentlewomen I told you of—Lord, they have
the oddest diversions—would never let me rest till I promised to go with them to the markets this morning to eat
fruit and buy nosegays.   30

MRS. LOVEIT.

Are they so fond of a filthy nosegay?

BELLINDA.

They complain of the stinks of the town and are never well
but when they have their noses in one.

MRS. LOVEIT.

There are essences and sweet waters.

BELLINDA.

Oh, they cry out upon perfumes, they are unwholesome.   35
One of 'em was falling into a fit with the smell of these
narolii.

MRS. LOVEIT.

Methinks, in complaisance you should have had a nosegay
too.

BELLINDA.

Do you think, my dear, I could be so loathsome to trick   40
myself up with carnations and stock-gillyflowers? I begged
their pardon and told them I never wore anything but
orange-flowers and tuberose. That which made me willing
to go was a strange desire I had to eat some fresh nectarines.

MRS. LOVEIT.

And had you any?   45

---

37. *narolii*] essences of orange; the word usually occurs in the singular
form and with the spelling *neroli* or *neroly.*
41. *stock-gillyflowers*] carnation-like flowers.
43. *tuberose*] plant with white, lily-like flowers.

BELLINDA.

The best I ever tasted.

MRS. LOVEIT.

Whence came you now?

BELLINDA.

From their lodgings, where I crowded out of a coach and took a chair to come and see you, my dear.

MRS. LOVEIT.

Whither did you send for that chair?   50

BELLINDA.

'Twas going by empty.

MRS. LOVEIT.

Where do these country gentlewomen lodge, I pray?

BELLINDA.

In the Strand, over against the Exchange.

PERT.

That place is never without a nest of 'em. They are always, as one goes by, fleering in balconies or staring out of   55
windows.

Enter Footman.

MRS. LOVEIT (*to the* Footman).

Come hither.   *Whispers.*

BELLINDA (*aside*).

This fellow by her order has been questioning the chairmen.
I threatened 'em with the name of Dorimant. If they should
have told truth, I am lost forever.   60

MRS. LOVEIT.

In the Strand, said you?

FOOTMAN.

Yes, madam, over against the Exchange.   *Exit* Footman.

MRS. LOVEIT.

She's innocent, and I am much to blame.

BELLINDA (*aside*).

I am so frighted, my countenance will betray me.

MRS. LOVEIT.

Bellinda, what makes you look so pale?   65

BELLINDA.

Want of my usual rest and jolting up and down so long in an odious hackney.

---

55. *fleering*] jeering; cf. III.i.125.

Footman returns.

FOOTMAN.

　　Madam, Mr. Dorimant.　　　　　　　　[*Exit* Footman.]

MRS. LOVEIT.

　　What makes him here?

BELLINDA (*aside*).

　　Then I am betrayed indeed. H' has broke his word, and I　70
love a man that does not care for me.

MRS. LOVEIT.

　　Lord, you faint, Bellinda.

BELLINDA.

　　I think I shall—such an oppression here on the sudden.

PERT.

　　She has eaten too much fruit, I warrant you.

MRS. LOVEIT.

　　Not unlikely.　　　　　　　　　　　　　　　　　　75

PERT.

　　'Tis that lies heavy on her stomach.

MRS. LOVEIT.

　　Have her into my chamber, give her some surfeit-water, and
let her lie down a little.

PERT.

　　Come, madam. I was a strange devourer of fruit when I was
young—so ravenous.　　　　　　　　　　　　　　　　80

　　　　　　　　Exeunt Bellinda *and* Pert, *leading her off.*

MRS. LOVEIT.

　　Oh, that my love would be but calm awhile, that I might
receive this man with all the scorn and indignation he
deserves!

　　　　　　　　　　Enter Dorimant.

DORIMANT.

　　Now for a touch of Sir Fopling to begin with. —Hey, page!
Give positive order that none of my people stir. Let the　85
canaille wait, as they should do. —Since noise and nonsense

70. *H' has*] Q*1–3;* H'as *1704.*

---

69. *What . . . here*] What brings him here?
77. *surfeit-water*] medicinal drink.
79. *strange*] great, immoderate.
86. *canaille*] rabble.

have such pow'rful charms,
       "I, that I may successful prove,
           Transform myself to what you love."

MRS. LOVEIT.

If that would do, you need not change from what you are: 90
you can be vain and loud enough.

DORIMANT.

But not with so good a grace as Sir Fopling. —"Hey,
Hampshire!"—Oh, that sound! That sound becomes the
mouth of a man of quality.

MRS. LOVEIT.

Is there a thing so hateful as a senseless mimic?   95

DORIMANT.

He's a great grievance, indeed, to all who—like yourself,
madam—love to play the fool in quiet.

MRS. LOVEIT.

A ridiculous animal, who has more of the ape than the ape
has of the man in him.

DORIMANT.

I have as mean an opinion of a sheer mimic as yourself; yet 100
were he all ape, I should prefer him to the gay, the giddy,
brisk, insipid, noisy fool you dote on.

MRS. LOVEIT.

Those noisy fools, however you despise 'em, have good
qualities which weigh more (or ought, at least) with us
women than all the pernicious wit you have to boast of.   105

DORIMANT.

That I may hereafter have a just value for their merit, pray
do me the favor to name 'em.

MRS. LOVEIT.

You'll despise 'em as the dull effects of ignorance and
vanity, yet I care not if I mention some. First, they really
admire us, while you at best but flatter us well.   110

DORIMANT.

Take heed; fools can dissemble too.

MRS. LOVEIT.

They may—but not so artificially as you. There is no fear

88–89. *I . . . love*] Waller, "To the Mutable Fair," ll. 5–6 (Thorn Drury,
I, 106). Dorimant substitutes *I, that* for the original "And, that."

they should deceive us. Then, they are assiduous, sir. They
are ever offering us their service and always waiting on our
will.   115

DORIMANT.

You owe that to their excessive idleness. They know not
how to entertain themselves at home, and find so little welcome abroad, they are fain to fly to you who countenance
'em, as a refuge against the solitude they would be otherwise condemned to.   120

MRS. LOVEIT.

Their conversation, too, diverts us better.

DORIMANT.

Playing with your fan, smelling to your gloves, commend-
ing your hair, and taking notice how 'tis cut and shaded
after the new way—

MRS. LOVEIT.

Were it sillier than you can make it, you must allow 'tis   125
pleasanter to laugh at others than to be laughed at ourselves, though never so wittily. Then, though they want
skill to flatter us, they flatter themselves so well, they save
us the labor. We need not take that care and pains to satisfy
'em of our love, which we so often lose on you.   130

DORIMANT.

They commonly, indeed, believe too well of themselves—
and always better of you than you deserve.

MRS. LOVEIT.

You are in the right: they have an implicit faith in us,
which keeps 'em from prying narrowly into our secrets and
saves us the vexatious trouble of clearing doubts which your   135
subtle and causeless jealousies every moment raise.

DORIMANT.

There is an inbred falsehood in women which inclines 'em
still to them whom they may most easily deceive.

MRS. LOVEIT.

The man who loves above his quality does not suffer more
from the insolent impertinence of his mistress than the   140
woman who loves above her understanding does from the
arrogant presumptions of her friend.

DORIMANT.

You mistake the use of fools: they are designed for proper-

ties and not for friends. You have an indifferent stock of
reputation left yet. Lose it all like a frank gamester on the 145
square. 'Twill then be time enough to turn rook and cheat
it up again on a good, substantial bubble.

MRS. LOVEIT.

The old and the ill-favored are only fit for properties,
indeed; but young and handsome fools have met with
kinder fortunes.   150

DORIMANT.

They have, to the shame of your sex be it spoken. 'Twas
this, the thought of this, made me by a timely jealousy
endeavor to prevent the good fortune you are providing for
Sir Fopling. But against a woman's frailty all our care is vain.

MRS. LOVEIT.

Had I not with a dear experience bought the knowledge of 155
your falsehood, you might have fooled me yet. This is not
the first jealousy you have feigned to make a quarrel with
me, and get a week to throw away on some such unknown,
inconsiderable slut as you have been lately lurking with at
plays.   160

DORIMANT.

Women, when they would break off with a man, never want
th'address to turn the fault on him.

MRS. LOVEIT.

You take a pride of late in using of me ill, that the town
may know the power you have over me, which now (as
unreasonably as yourself) expects that I, do me all the 165
injuries you can, must love you still.

DORIMANT.

I am so far from expecting that you should, I begin to think
you never did love me.

MRS. LOVEIT.

Would the memory of it were so wholly worn out in me that
I did doubt it too. What made you come to disturb my 170
growing quiet?

145. yet] *Q1–2, 1704;* you *Q3.*   161. never] *Q1, 1704;* ne'er *Q2–3.*

---

144. *indifferent*] moderate.
146. *rook*] sharper.
147. *bubble*] dupe, gull.

DORIMANT.

To give you joy of your growing infamy.

MRS. LOVEIT.

Insupportable! Insulting devil! This from you, the only
author of my shame! This from another had been justice;
but from you, 'tis a hellish and inhuman outrage. What 175
have I done?

DORIMANT.

A thing that puts you below my scorn and makes my anger
as ridiculous as you have made my love.

MRS. LOVEIT.

I walked last night with Sir Fopling.

DORIMANT.

You did, madam; and you talked and laughed aloud, "Ha, 180
ha, ha." Oh, that laugh! That laugh becomes the confidence
of a woman of quality.

MRS. LOVEIT.

You, who have more pleasure in the ruin of a woman's
reputation than in the endearments of her love, reproach
me not with yourself and I defy you to name the man can 185
lay a blemish on my fame.

DORIMANT.

To be seen publicly so transported with the vain follies of
that notorious fop, to me is an infamy below the sin of
prostitution with another man.

MRS. LOVEIT.

Rail on! I am satisfied in the justice of what I did: you had 190
provoked me to it.

DORIMANT.

What I did was the effect of a passion whose extravagancies
you have been willing to forgive.

MRS. LOVEIT.

And what I did was the effect of a passion you may forgive
if you think fit.   195

DORIMANT.

Are you so indifferent grown?

MRS. LOVEIT.

I am.

DORIMANT.

Nay, then 'tis time to part. I'll send you back your letters

you have so often asked for. [*Looks in his pockets.*]   I have
two or three of 'em about me.   200

MRS. LOVEIT.

Give 'em me.

DORIMANT.

You snatch as if you thought I would not.

[*Gives her the letters.*]

There. And may the perjuries in 'em be mine if e'er I see
you more.   *Offers to go; she catches him.*

MRS. LOVEIT.

Stay!   205

DORIMANT.

I will not.

MRS. LOVEIT.

You shall!

DORIMANT.

What have you to say?

MRS. LOVEIT.

I cannot speak it yet.

DORIMANT.

Something more in commendation of the fool. Death, I 210
want patience! Let me go.

MRS. LOVEIT.

I cannot. (*Aside.*)   I can sooner part with the limbs that
hold him. —I hate that nauseous fool, you know I do.

DORIMANT.

Was it the scandal you were fond of, then?

MRS. LOVEIT.

Y' had raised my anger equal to my love, a thing you ne'er 215
could do before; and in revenge I did—I know not what I
did. Would you would not think on't any more.

DORIMANT.

Should I be willing to forget it, I shall be daily minded of it.
'Twill be a commonplace for all the town to laugh at me,
and Medley, when he is rhetorically drunk, will ever be 220
declaiming on it in my ears.

214. Was] *Q1–2, 1704;* Were *Q3.*   221. on] *Q1–2, 1704;* of *Q3.*

MRS. LOVEIT.

'Twill be believed a jealous spite. Come, forget it.

DORIMANT.

Let me consult my reputation; you are too careless of it. (*Pauses.*) You shall meet Sir Fopling in the Mail again tonight.   225

MRS. LOVEIT.

What mean you?

DORIMANT.

I have thought on it, and you must. 'Tis necessary to justify my love to the world. You can handle a coxcomb as he deserves when you are not out of humor, madam.

MRS. LOVEIT.

Public satisfaction for the wrong I have done you? This is 230 some new device to make me more ridiculous.

DORIMANT.

Hear me.

MRS. LOVEIT.

I will not.

DORIMANT.

You will be persuaded.

MRS. LOVEIT.

Never!   235

DORIMANT.

Are you so obstinate?

MRS. LOVEIT.

Are you so base?

DORIMANT.

You will not satisfy my love?

MRS. LOVEIT.

I would die to satisfy that; but I will not, to save you from a thousand racks, do a shameless thing to please your 240 vanity.

DORIMANT.

Farewell, false woman.

MRS. LOVEIT.

Do! Go!

223. too] *Q1, Q3, 1704;* to *Q2.*   227. on it] *Q1;* on't *Q2–3, 1704.*

DORIMANT.

You will call me back again.

MRS. LOVEIT.

Exquisite fiend! I knew you came but to torment me.   245

Enter Bellinda *and* Pert.

DORIMANT (*surprised*).

Bellinda here!

BELLINDA (*aside*).

He starts and looks pale. The sight of me has touched his
guilty soul.

PERT.

'Twas but a qualm, as I said, a little indigestion. The surfeit-
water did it, madam, mixed with a little mirabilis.   250

DORIMANT [*aside*].

I am confounded, and cannot guess how she came hither.

MRS. LOVEIT.

'Tis your fortune, Bellinda, ever to be here when I am
abused by this prodigy of ill nature.

BELLINDA.

I am amazed to find him here. How has he the face to come
near you?   255

DORIMANT [*aside*].

Here is fine work towards! I never was at such a loss before.

BELLINDA.

One who makes a public profession of breach of faith and
ingratitude—I loathe the sight of him.

DORIMANT [*aside*].

There is no remedy. I must submit to their tongues now and
some other time bring myself off as well as I can.   260

BELLINDA.

Other men are wicked, but then they have some sense of
shame. He is never well but when he triumphs—nay, glories
—to a woman's face in his villainies.

MRS. LOVEIT.

You are in the right, Bellinda; but methinks your kindness
for me makes you concern yourself too much with him.   265

---

250. *mirabilis*] aqua mirabilis; medicinal drink of wine and spices.

BELLINDA.

It does indeed, my dear. His barbarous carriage to you yesterday made me hope you ne'er would see him more, and the
very next day to find him here again provokes me strangely.
But because I know you love him, I have done.

DORIMANT.

You have reproached me handsomely, and I deserve it for 270
coming hither, but—

PERT.

You must expect it, sir. All women will hate you for my
lady's sake.

DORIMANT (aside).

Nay, if she begins too, 'tis time to fly. I shall be scolded to
death, else. (To Bellinda.) I am to blame in some cir- 275
cumstances, I confess; but as to the main, I am not so
guilty as you imagine. [Aloud.] I shall seek a more
convenient time to clear myself.

MRS. LOVEIT.

Do it now! What impediments are here?

DORIMANT.

I want time, and you want temper. 280

MRS. LOVEIT.

These are weak pretenses.

DORIMANT.

You were never more mistaken in your life; and so farewell.

Dorimant flings off.

MRS. LOVEIT.

Call a footman, Pert. Quickly! I will have him dogged.

PERT.

I wish you would not, for my quiet and your own.

MRS. LOVEIT.

I'll find out the infamous cause of all our quarrels, pluck 285
her mask off, and expose her bare-faced to the world!

[*Exit* Pert.]

BELLINDA (aside).

Let me but escape this time, I'll never venture more.

MRS. LOVEIT.

Bellinda, you shall go with me.

268. here] Q1, 1704; Q2–3 omit.

BELLINDA.

I have such a heaviness hangs on me with what I did this
morning, I would fain go home and sleep, my dear.   290
MRS. LOVEIT.

Death and eternal darkness! I shall never sleep again.
Raging fevers seize the world and make mankind as restless
all as I am!   *Exit* Mrs. Loveit.
BELLINDA.

I knew him false and helped to make him so. Was not her
ruin enough to fright me from the danger? It should have 295
been, but love can take no warning.   *Exit* Bellinda.

[V.ii]

Lady Townley's house. Enter Medley, Young Bellair, Lady Townley,
Emilia, *and* [Smirk, *a*] *chaplain.*

MEDLEY.

Bear up, Bellair, and do not let us see that repentance in
thine we daily do in married faces.
LADY TOWNLEY.

This wedding will strangely surprise my brother when he
knows it.
MEDLEY.

Your nephew ought to conceal it for a time, madam. Since   5
marriage has lost its good name, prudent men seldom expose
their own reputations till 'tis convenient to justify their
wives'.
OLD BELLAIR (*without*).

Where are you all there? Out, adod, will nobody hear?
LADY TOWNLEY.

My brother! Quickly, Mr. Smirk, into this closet. You must 10
not be seen yet.   [Smirk] *goes into the closet.*

Enter Old Bellair *and Lady Townley's Page.*

OLD BELLAIR [*to Page*].

Desire Mr. Fourbe to walk into the lower parlor. I will be

---

289. *heaviness*] drowsiness.
[V.ii]
10. *closet*] small inner room.

with him presently.   [*Exit Page.*]

(*To* Young Bellair.)   Where have you been, sir, you could
not wait on me today?   15

YOUNG BELLAIR.

About a business.

OLD BELLAIR.

Are you so good at business? Adod, I have a business too,
you shall dispatch out of hand, sir. —Send for a parson,
sister. My Lady Woodvill and her daughter are coming.

LADY TOWNLEY.

What need you huddle up things thus?   20

OLD BELLAIR.

Out a pize! Youth is apt to play the fool, and 'tis not good it
should be in their power.

LADY TOWNLEY.

You need not fear your son.

OLD BELLAIR.

H' has been idling this morning, and adod, I do not like
him. (*To* Emilia.)   How dost thou do, sweetheart?   25

EMILIA.

You are very severe, sir. Married in such haste!

OLD BELLAIR.

Go to, thou'rt a rogue, and I will talk with thee anon.

Enter Lady Woodvill, Harriet, *and* Busy.

Here's my Lady Woodvill come. —Welcome, madam. Mr.
Fourbe's below with the writings.

LADY WOODVILL.

Let us down and make an end, then.   30

OLD BELLAIR.

Sister, show the way. (*To* Young Bellair, *who is talking to*
Harriet.)   Harry, your business lies not there yet. —Excuse
him till we have done, lady, and then, adod, he shall be for
thee. —Mr. Medley, we must trouble you to be a witness.

27. to] *D, Verity; too Q1–3, 1704,*   27. thou'rt] *Q1, 1704;* thou art
Brett-Smith.   *Q2–3.*

---

20. *huddle up*] rush.
27. *Go to*] "Go along."
29. *writings*] i.e., documents of the marriage settlement.

MEDLEY.

    I luckily came for that purpose, sir.   35

Exeunt Old Bellair, Medley, Young Bellair, Lady Townley, *and* Lady Woodvill.

BUSY [*to* Harriet].

    What will you do, madam?

HARRIET.

    Be carried back and mewed up in the country again, run away here—anything rather than be married to a man I do not care for. —Dear Emilia, do thou advise me.

EMILIA.

    Mr. Bellair is engaged, you know.   40

HARRIET.

    I do, but know not what the fear of losing an estate may fright him to.

EMILIA.

    In the desp'rate condition you are in, you should consult with some judicious man. What think you of Mr. Dorimant?

HARRIET.

    I do not think of him at all.   45

BUSY [*aside*].

    She thinks of nothing else, I am sure.

EMILIA.

    How fond your mother was of Mr. Courtage.

HARRIET.

    Because I contrived the mistake to make a little mirth, you believe I like the man.

EMILIA.

    Mr. Bellair believes you love him.   50

HARRIET.

    Men are seldom in the right when they guess at a woman's mind. Would she whom he loves loved him no better!

BUSY (*aside*).

    That's e'en well enough, on all conscience.

EMILIA.

    Mr. Dorimant has a great deal of wit.

HARRIET.

    And takes a great deal of pains to show it.   55

---

37. *mewed up*] cooped up.

EMILIA.

    He's extremely well-fashioned.

HARRIET.

    Affectedly grave, or ridiculously wild and apish.

BUSY.

    You defend him still against your mother.

HARRIET.

    I would not, were he justly rallied; but I cannot hear any-
one undeservedly railed at.   60

EMILIA.

    Has your woman learnt the song you were so taken with?

HARRIET.

    I was fond of a new thing. 'Tis dull at second hearing.

EMILIA.

    Mr. Dorimant made it.

BUSY.

    She knows it, madam, and has made me sing it at least a
dozen times this morning.   65

HARRIET.

    Thy tongue is as impertinent as thy fingers.

EMILIA [to Busy].

    You have provoked her.

BUSY.

    'Tis but singing the song and I shall appease her.

EMILIA.

    Prithee, do.

HARRIET.

    She has a voice will grate your ears worse than a catcall,   70
and dresses so ill she's scarce fit to trick up a yeoman's
daughter on a holiday.

Busy sings.

Song, by Sir C. S.

As Amoret with Phillis sat
One evening on the plain,

73. sat] *Q1, 1704;* sate *Q2–3.*

    72.2. *Sir C. S.*] probably Sir Car Scroope, who wrote the prologue
(though the initials are also those of Sir Charles Sedley). The song imitates
a French original; see Brett-Smith, pp. 323–324.

And saw the charming Strephon wait   75
  To tell the nymph his pain,

The threat'ning danger to remove,
  She whispered in her ear,
"Ah, Phillis, if you would not love,
  This shepherd do not hear: 80

None ever had so strange an art,
  His passion to convey
Into a list'ning virgin's heart
  And steal her soul away.

Fly, fly betimes, for fear you give   85
  Occasion for your fate."
"In vain," said she, "in vain I strive.
  Alas, 'tis now too late."

Enter Dorimant.

DORIMANT.
  "Music so softens and disarms the mind—"
HARRIET.
  "That not one arrow does resistance find."   90
DORIMANT.
  Let us make use of the lucky minute, then.
HARRIET (*aside, turning from* Dorimant).
  My love springs with my blood into my face. I dare not look
  upon him yet.
DORIMANT.
  What have we here—the picture of a celebrated beauty
  giving audience in public to a declared lover?   95
HARRIET.
  Play the dying fop and make the piece complete, sir.
DORIMANT.
  What think you if the hint were well improved—the whole

94. a celebrated] *CBEP, Brett-
Smith;* celebrated *Q 1–3, 1704.*

_____

85. *betimes*] in time.
89–90. *Music . . . find*] Waller, "Of my Lady Isabella, Playing on the
Lute," ll. 11–12 (Thorn Drury, I, 90). Harriet substitutes *one* for the
original "an."

mystery of making love pleasantly designed and wrought in
a suit of hangings?

HARRIET.

'Twere needless to execute fools in effigy who suffer daily in   100
their own persons.

DORIMANT (*to* Emilia, *aside*).

Mrs. Bride, for such I know this happy day has made you—

EMILIA.

Defer the formal joy you are to give me, and mind your
business with her. (*Aloud.*) Here are dreadful prepara-
tions, Mr. Dorimant—writings sealing, and a parson sent   105
for.

DORIMANT.

To marry this lady?

BUSY.

Condemned she is; and what will become of her I know not,
without you generously engage in a rescue.

DORIMANT.

In this sad condition, madam, I can do no less than offer   110
you my service.

HARRIET.

The obligation is not great: you are the common sanctuary
for all young women who run from their relations.

DORIMANT.

I have always my arms open to receive the distressed. But I
will open my heart and receive you where none yet did   115
ever enter. You have filled it with a secret, might I but let
you know it.

HARRIET.

Do not speak it if you would have me believe it. Your
tongue is so famed for falsehood, 'twill do the truth an
injury.   *Turns away her head.*   120

DORIMANT.

Turn not away, then, but look on me and guess it.

HARRIET.

Did you not tell me there was no credit to be given to faces
—that women nowadays have their passions as much at will
as they have their complexions, and put on joy and sadness,

99. *suit*] set.

scorn and kindness, with the same ease they do their paint 125
and patches? Are they the only counterfeits?

DORIMANT.

You wrong your own while you suspect my eyes. By all the
hope I have in you, the inimitable color in your cheeks is
not more free from art than are the sighs I offer.

HARRIET.

In men who have been long hardened in sin, we have reason 130
to mistrust the first signs of repentance.

DORIMANT.

The prospect of such a heav'n will make me persevere and
give you marks that are infallible.

HARRIET.

What are those?

DORIMANT.

I will renounce all the joys I have in friendship and in wine, 135
sacrifice to you all the interest I have in other women—

HARRIET.

Hold! Though I wish you devout, I would not have you
turn fanatic. Could you neglect these a while and make a
journey into the country?

DORIMANT.

To be with you, I could live there and never send one 140
thought to London.

HARRIET.

Whate'er you say, I know all beyond High Park's a desert
to you, and that no gallantry can draw you farther.

DORIMANT.

That has been the utmost limit of my love; but now my
passion knows no bounds, and there's no measure to be taken 145
of what I'll do for you from anything I ever did before.

HARRIET.

When I hear you talk thus in Hampshire, I shall begin to
think there may be some little truth enlarged upon.

DORIMANT.

Is this all? Will you not promise me—

148. little] *Q1 (some copies); Q2-3,*
1704 omit.

HARRIET.

> I hate to promise. What we do then is expected from us 150
> and wants much of the welcome it finds when it surprises.

DORIMANT.

> May I not hope?

HARRIET.

> That depends on you and not on me; and 'tis to no purpose
> to forbid it.   *Turns to* Busy.

BUSY.

> Faith, madam, now I perceive the gentleman loves you too. 155
> E'en let him know your mind, and torment yourselves no
> longer.

HARRIET.

> Dost think I have no sense of modesty?

BUSY.

> Think, if you lose this, you may never have another
> opportunity.   160

HARRIET.

> May he hate me—a curse that frights me when I speak it—
> if ever I do a thing against the rules of decency and honor.

DORIMANT (*to* Emilia).

> I am beholding to you for your good intentions, madam.

EMILIA.

> I thought the concealing of our marriage from her might
> have done you better service.   165

DORIMANT.

> Try her again.

EMILIA [*to* Harriet].

> What have you resolved, madam? The time draws near.

HARRIET.

> To be obstinate and protest against this marriage.

> > *Enter* Lady Townley *in haste.*

LADY TOWNLEY (*to* Emilia).

> Quickly, quickly, let Mr. Smirk out of the closet!

> > Smirk *comes out of the closet.*

HARRIET.

> A parson! [*To* Dorimant.] Had you laid him in here? 170

DORIMANT.

> I knew nothing of him.

HARRIET.

Should it appear you did, your opinion of my easiness may
cost you dear.

Enter Old Bellair, Young Bellair, Medley, *and* Lady Woodvill.

OLD BELLAIR.

Out a pize, the canonical hour is almost past! Sister, is the
man of God come?   175

LADY TOWNLEY [*indicating* Smirk].

He waits your leisure.

OLD BELLAIR [*to* Smirk].

By your favor, sir. —Adod, a pretty spruce fellow. What
may we call him?

LADY TOWNLEY.

Mr. Smirk—my Lady Biggot's chaplain.

OLD BELLAIR.

A wise woman, adod she is; the man will serve for the flesh 180
as well as the spirit. —Please you, sir, to commission a young
couple to go to bed together a God's name?—Harry!

YOUNG BELLAIR.

Here, sir.

OLD BELLAIR.

Out a pize! Without your mistress in your hand?

SMIRK.

Is this the gentleman?   185

OLD BELLAIR.

Yes, sir.

SMIRK.

Are you not mistaken, sir?

OLD BELLAIR.

Adod, I think not, sir!

SMIRK.

Sure you are, sir.

OLD BELLAIR.

You look as if you would forbid the banns, Mr. Smirk. I   190
hope you have no pretension to the lady.

---

174. *canonical hour*] time during which marriages could be legally performed.

SMIRK.

Wish him joy, sir. I have done him the good office today already.

OLD BELLAIR.

Out a pize! What do I hear?

LADY TOWNLEY.

Never storm, brother. The truth is out.   195

OLD BELLAIR.

How say you, sir? Is this your wedding day?

YOUNG BELLAIR.

It is, sir.

OLD BELLAIR.

And, adod, it shall be mine too. (*To* Emilia.) Give me thy hand, sweetheart. [*She refuses.*] What dost thou mean? Give me thy hand, I say!   200

Emilia *kneels and* Young Bellair.

LADY TOWNLEY.

Come, come, give her your blessing. This is the woman your son loved and is married to.

OLD BELLAIR.

Ha! Cheated! Cozened! And by your contrivance, sister!

LADY TOWNLEY.

What would you do with her? She's a rogue, and you can't abide her.   205

MEDLEY.

Shall I hit her a pat for you, sir?

OLD BELLAIR.

Adod, you are all rogues, and I never will forgive you.

[*Flings away, as if to exit.*]

LADY TOWNLEY.

Whither? Whither away?

MEDLEY.

Let him go and cool awhile.

LADY WOODVILL (*to* Dorimant).

Here's a business broke out now, Mr. Courtage. I am made 210 a fine fool of.

DORIMANT.

You see the old gentleman knew nothing of it.

212. knew] *Q1–3;* knows *1704.*

LADY WOODVILL.

I find he did not. I shall have some trick put upon me, if I
stay in this wicked town any longer. —Harriet, dear child,
where art thou? I'll into the country straight.   215

OLD BELLAIR.

Adod, madam, you shall hear me first.

Enter Mrs. Loveit *and* Bellinda.

MRS. LOVEIT.

Hither my man dogged him.

BELLINDA.

Yonder he stands, my dear.

MRS. LOVEIT.

I see him, (*aside*) and with him the face that has undone me.
Oh, that I were but where I might throw out the anguish of 220
my heart! Here it must rage within and break it.

LADY TOWNLEY.

Mrs. Loveit! Are you afraid to come forward?

MRS. LOVEIT.

I was amazed to see so much company here in a morning.
The occasion sure is extraordinary.

DORIMANT (*aside*).

Loveit and Bellinda! The devil owes me a shame today, and 225
I think never will have done paying it.

MRS. LOVEIT.

Married! Dear Emilia, how am I transported with the news!

HARRIET (*to* Dorimant).

I little thought Emilia was the woman Mr. Bellair was in
love with. I'll chide her for not trusting me with the secret.

DORIMANT.

How do you like Mrs. Loveit?   230

HARRIET.

She's a famed mistress of yours, I hear.

DORIMANT.

She has been, on occasion.

---

219. with him] *Q1–3; 1704 omits*   231. mistress] *1704; Q1–3 print*
him.   Mrs.

225–226. *The devil . . . it*] Dorimant varies a proverb that "the devil
owed (one) a shame and now has paid it" (Tilley, pp. 152–153).

OLD BELLAIR (*to* Lady Woodvill).

Adod, madam, I cannot help it.

LADY WOODVILL.

You need make no more apologies, sir.

EMILIA (*to* Mrs. Loveit).

The old gentleman's excusing himself to my Lady Woodvill. 235

MRS. LOVEIT.

Ha, ha, ha! I never heard of anything so pleasant.

HARRIET (*to* Dorimant).

She's extremely overjoyed at something.

DORIMANT.

At nothing. She is one of those hoiting ladies who gaily fling themselves about and force a laugh when their aching hearts are full of discontent and malice.   240

MRS. LOVEIT.

Oh heav'n, I was never so near killing myself with laughing.
—Mr. Dorimant, are you a brideman?

LADY WOODVILL.

Mr. Dorimant! Is this Mr. Dorimant, madam?

MRS. LOVEIT.

If you doubt it, your daughter can resolve you, I suppose.

LADY WOODVILL.

I am cheated too, basely cheated!   245

OLD BELLAIR.

Out a pize, what's here? More knavery yet?

LADY WOODVILL.

Harriet! On my blessing, come away, I charge you.

HARRIET.

Dear mother, do but stay and hear me.

LADY WOODVILL.

I am betrayed! And thou art undone, I fear.

HARRIET.

Do not fear it. I have not, nor never will, do anything 250
against my duty. Believe me, dear mother, do!

DORIMANT (*to* Mrs. Loveit).

I had trusted you with this secret but that I knew the
violence of your nature would ruin my fortune—as now

---

238. *hoiting*] giddy.

unluckily it has. I thank you, madam.

MRS. LOVEIT.

She's an heiress, I know, and very rich.   255

DORIMANT.

To satisfy you, I must give up my interest wholly to my love.
Had you been a reasonable woman, I might have secured
'em both and been happy.

MRS. LOVEIT.

You might have trusted me with anything of this kind; you
know you might. Why did you go under a wrong name?   260

DORIMANT.

The story is too long to tell you now. Be satisfied; this is the
business, this is the mask has kept me from you.

BELLINDA (aside).

He's tender of my honor, though he's cruel to my love.

MRS. LOVEIT.

Was it no idle mistress, then?

DORIMANT.

Believe me—a wife, to repair the ruins of my estate that 265
needs it.

MRS. LOVEIT.

The knowledge of this makes my grief hang lighter on my
soul, but I shall never more be happy.

DORIMANT.

Bellinda—

BELLINDA.

Do not think of clearing yourself with me. It is impossible. 270
Do all men break their words thus?

DORIMANT.

Th'extravagant words they speak in love. 'Tis as unreasonable to expect we should perform all we promise then,
as do all we threaten when we are angry. When I see you
next—   275

BELLINDA.

Take no notice of me, and I shall not hate you.

DORIMANT.

How came you to Mrs. Loveit?

258. 'em] *Q 1–2, 1704;* 'm *Q 3.*

BELLINDA.

By a mistake the chairmen made for want of my giving them
directions.

DORIMANT.

'Twas a pleasant one. We must meet again.   280

BELLINDA.

Never.

DORIMANT.

Never?

BELLINDA.

When we do, may I be as infamous as you are false.

LADY TOWNLEY [to Lady Woodvill].

Men of Mr. Dorimant's character always suffer in the
general opinion of the world.   285

MEDLEY.

You can make no judgment of a witty man from common
fame, considering the prevailing faction, madam.

OLD BELLAIR.

Adod, he's in the right.

MEDLEY.

Besides, 'tis a common error among women to believe too
well of them they know and too ill of them they don't.   290

OLD BELLAIR.

Adod, he observes well.

LADY TOWNLEY.

Believe me, madam, you will find Mr. Dorimant as civil a
gentleman as you thought Mr. Courtage.

HARRIET.

If you would but know him better—

LADY WOODVILL.

You have a mind to know him better? Come away! You   295
shall never see him more.

HARRIET.

Dear mother, stay!

LADY WOODVILL.

I wo' not be consenting to your ruin.

HARRIET.

Were my fortune in your power—

282. Never?] *Verity;* Never! *Q1–3,*   294. would but] *Q1, 1704;* have
1704.   mind to *Q2;* have a mind to *Q3.*

LADY WOODVILL.

Your person is.   300

HARRIET.

Could I be disobedient, I might take it out of yours and put
it into his.

LADY WOODVILL.

'Tis that you would be at! You would marry this Dorimant!

HARRIET.

I cannot deny it. I would, and never will marry any other
man.   305

LADY WOODVILL.

Is this the duty that you promised?

HARRIET.

But I will never marry him against your will.

LADY WOODVILL (*aside*).

She knows the way to melt my heart. (*To* Harriet.)
Upon yourself light your undoing.

MEDLEY (*to* Old Bellair).

Come, sir, you have not the heart any longer to refuse your 310
blessing.

OLD BELLAIR.

Adod, I ha' not. —Rise, and God bless you both. Make
much of her, Harry; she deserves thy kindness. (*To*
Emilia.)   Adod, sirrah, I did not think it had been in thee.

Enter Sir Fopling *and's* Page.

SIR FOPLING.

'Tis a damned windy day. Hey, page! Is my periwig right? 315

PAGE.

A little out of order, sir.

SIR FOPLING.

Pox o' this apartment! It wants an antechamber to adjust
oneself in.   (*To* Mrs. Loveit.)   Madam, I came from your
house, and your servants directed me hither.

MRS. LOVEIT.

I will give order hereafter they shall direct you better.   320

SIR FOPLING.

The great satisfaction I had in the Mail last night has given
me much disquiet since.

MRS. LOVEIT.

'Tis likely to give me more than I desire.

SIR FOPLING [*aside*].

What the devil makes her so reserved?—Am I guilty of an
indiscretion, madam? 325

MRS. LOVEIT.

You will be of a great one, if you continue your mistake, sir.

SIR FOPLING.

Something puts you out of humor.

MRS. LOVEIT.

The most foolish, inconsiderable thing that ever did.

SIR FOPLING.

Is it in my power?

MRS. LOVEIT.

To hang or drown it. Do one of 'em, and trouble me no 330
more.

SIR FOPLING.

So *fière*? *Serviteur*, madam. —Medley, where's Dorimant?

MEDLEY.

Methinks the lady has not made you those advances today
she did last night, Sir Fopling.

SIR FOPLING.

Prithee, do not talk of her. 335

MEDLEY.

She would be a *bonne fortune*.

SIR FOPLING.

Not to me at present.

MEDLEY.

How so?

SIR FOPLING.

An intrigue now would be but a temptation to me to throw
away that vigor on one which I mean shall shortly make my 340
court to the whole sex in a ballet.

MEDLEY.

Wisely considered, Sir Fopling.

SIR FOPLING.

No one woman is worth the loss of a cut in a caper.

MEDLEY.

Not when 'tis so universally designed.

---

332. *fière*] haughty.   332. *Serviteur*] your servant.
343. *cut*] rapid back-and-forth movement of the feet during a high leap.

LADY WOODVILL.

Mr. Dorimant, everyone has spoke so much in your behalf 345
that I can no longer doubt but I was in the wrong.

MRS. LOVEIT [*to* Bellinda].

There's nothing but falsehood and impertinence in this
world. All men are villains or fools. Take example from my
misfortunes. Bellinda, if thou wouldst be happy, give thyself
wholly up to goodness.   350

HARRIET (*to* Mrs. Loveit).

Mr. Dorimant has been your God almighty long enough.
'Tis time to think of another.

MRS. LOVEIT [*to* Bellinda].

Jeered by her! I will lock myself up in my house and never
see the world again.

HARRIET.

A nunnery is the more fashionable place for such a retreat 355
and has been the fatal consequence of many a *belle passion*.

MRS. LOVEIT [*aside*].

Hold, heart, till I get home! Should I answer, 'twould make
her triumph greater.   *Is going out.*

DORIMANT.

Your hand, Sir Fopling—

SIR FOPLING.

Shall I wait upon you, madam?   360

MRS. LOVEIT.

Legion of fools, as many devils take thee!

Exit Mrs. Loveit.

MEDLEY.

Dorimant, I pronounce thy reputation clear; and henceforward, when I would know anything of woman, I will
consult no other oracle.

SIR FOPLING.

Stark mad, by all that's handsome! —Dorimant, thou hast 365
engaged me in a pretty business.

349. misfortunes. Bellinda,] *Q 1–3,*   *Brett-Smith.*
1704; misfortunes, Bellinda; *Verity,*

356. *belle passion*] violent passion.
361. *Legion . . . thee*] with an echo of Mark 5:9; cf. Epilogue, l. 18.

DORIMANT.

I have not leisure now to talk about it.

OLD BELLAIR.

Out a pize, what does this man of mode do here again?

LADY TOWNLEY.

He'll be an excellent entertainment within, brother, and is
luckily come to raise the mirth of the company.   370

LADY WOODVILL.

Madam, I take my leave of you.

LADY TOWNLEY.

What do you mean, madam?

LADY WOODVILL.

To go this afternoon part of my way to Hartly.

OLD BELLAIR.

Adod, you shall stay and dine first! Come, we will all be
good friends; and you shall give Mr. Dorimant leave to 375
wait upon you and your daughter in the country.

LADY WOODVILL.

If his occasions bring him that way, I have now so good an
opinion of him, he shall be welcome.

HARRIET.

To a great, rambling, lone house that looks as it were not
inhabited, the family's so small. There you'll find my 380
mother, an old lame aunt, and myself, sir, perched up on
chairs at a distance in a large parlor, sitting moping like
three or four melancholy birds in a spacious volary. Does not
this stagger your resolution?

DORIMANT.

Not at all, madam. The first time I saw you, you left me 385
with the pangs of love upon me; and this day my soul has
quite given up her liberty.

HARRIET.

This is more dismal than the country. —Emilia, pity me
who am going to that sad place. Methinks I hear the hateful
noise of rooks already—kaw, kaw, kaw. There's music in the 390

---

377. his] *Q1-2, 1704;* this *Q3.*   390. kaw, kaw, kaw] *Q1-3;* knaw,
                                             knaw, knaw *1704.*

---

373. *Hartly*] Hartley Row, Hampshire (?); otherwise, Lady Woodvill's
country estate.
383. *volary*] aviary.

worst cry in London. "My dill and cucumbers to pickle."

OLD BELLAIR.

Sister, knowing of this matter, I hope you have provided us
some good cheer.

LADY TOWNLEY.

I have, brother, and the fiddles too.

OLD BELLAIR.

Let 'em strike up then. The young lady shall have a dance 395
before she departs.

Dance.

(*After the dance.*)   So now we'll in, and make this an arrant
wedding day.

To the pit.

And if these honest gentlemen rejoice,
Adod, the boy has made a happy choice.   400

Exeunt omnes.

---

391. *cry*] street-vendor's cry.

THE EPILOGUE

By Mr. Dryden

Most modern wits such monstrous fools have shown,
They seemed not of heav'n's making, but their own.
Those nauseous harlequins in farce may pass,
But there goes more to a substantial ass;
Something of man must be exposed to view,   5
That, gallants, it may more resemble you.
Sir Fopling is a fool so nicely writ,
The ladies would mistake him for a wit
And when he sings, talks loud, and cocks, would cry:
"Ay, now methinks he's pretty company—   10
So brisk, so gay, so traveled, so refined,
As he took pains to graft upon his kind."
True fops help nature's work, and go to school
To file and finish God a'mighty's fool.
Yet none Sir Fopling him, or him, can call: 15
He's knight o' th' shire and represents ye all.
From each he meets, he culls whate'er he can;
Legion's his name, a people in a man.
His bulky folly gathers as it goes,
And, rolling o'er you, like a snowball grows.   20

6. it] *Brett-Smith;* they *Q 1–3, 1704.*
Brett-Smith follows a ms. version of the
epilogue, described by G. Thorn-Drury,
RES, I (July, 1925), 325–326.
10. Ay, now] I vow *Q 1–3, 1704;*
Brett-Smith follows the ms. I now *(for*
Ay, now *as here).*
14. *The ms. adds a couplet between*
ll. 14 and 15: Labor to put in more,
as Master Bayes/ Thrums in additions to his ten-years plays.

---

3. *harlequins*] Harlequin was a traditional figure of French and Italian
farce. Companies of traveling players from the continent had been well
received in England, to the displeasure of Dryden and others.
9. *cocks*] struts.
12. *As*] as if.
12. *to . . . kind*] to graft onto his own natural stock (of talents).
14–15.] See textual note. In the interpolated couplet Dryden turns the
tables on George Villiers, Duke of Buckingham, for his satiric portrait of
Dryden as Mr. Bayes in *The Rehearsal*; Buckingham's play was several
years in the making before its first performance in 1671 and was often
amended afterwards.
16. *knight o' th' shire*] parliamentary representative of a shire (county).

His various modes from various fathers follow;
One taught the toss, and one the new French wallow.
His sword-knot, this; his cravat, this designed;
And this, the yard-long snake he twirls behind.
From one, the sacred periwig he gained,   25
Which wind ne'er blew, nor touch of hat prophaned;
Another's diving bow he did adore,
Which with a shog casts all the hair before,
Till he with full decorum brings it back
And rises with a water spaniel shake.   30
As for his songs (the ladies' dear delight),
Those sure he took from most of you who write.
Yet every man is safe from what he feared,
For no one fool is hunted from the herd.

FINIS

---

22. *toss*] i.e., of the head.

22. *wallow*] cited by the *OED* as a sole instance of *wallow* in the meaning of "rolling walk or gait."

23. *sword-knot*] ribbon or tassel tied to a sword-hilt.

24. *snake*] curl or tail attached to a wig.

28. *shog*] shake.

Appendix

Chronology

Approximate years are indicated by *.

<table>
<tr><td>Political and Literary Events</td><td>Life and Major Works of Etherege</td></tr>
</table>

1631
Death of Donne.
John Dryden born.
Shirley's THE TRAITOR.

1633
Samuel Pepys born.

1635

George Etherege born.*

1640
Aphra Behn born.*

1641
William Wycherley born.*

1642
First Civil War began (ended 1646).
Theaters closed by Parliament.
Thomas Shadwell born.*

1648
Second Civil War.

1649
Execution of Charles I.

1650
Jeremy Collier born.

1651
Hobbes' *Leviathan* published.

1652
First Dutch War began (ended 1654).
Thomas Otway born.

1653
Nathaniel Lee born.*

1656
D'Avenant's *THE SIEGE OF RHODES* performed at Rutland House.

1657
John Dennis born.

1658
Death of Oliver Cromwell.
D'Avenant's *THE CRUELTY OF THE SPANIARDS IN PERU* performed at the Cockpit.

1660
Restoration of Charles II.
Theatrical patents granted to Thomas Killigrew and Sir William D'Avenant, authorizing them to form, respectively, the King's and the Duke of York's Companies.
Pepys began his diary.

1661
Cowley's *THE CUTTER OF COLEMAN STREET*.
D'Avenant's *THE SIEGE OF RHODES* (expanded to two parts).

1662
Charter granted to the Royal Society.

1663
Dryden's *THE WILD GALLANT*.
Tuke's *THE ADVENTURES OF FIVE HOURS*.

1664
Sir John Vanbrugh born.   *THE COMICAL REVENGE.*
Dryden's *THE RIVAL LADIES*.
Dryden and Howard's *THE INDIAN QUEEN*.

1665
Second Dutch War began (ended 1667).
Great Plague.

Dryden's *THE INDIAN EM-PEROR.*

Orrery's *MUSTAPHA.*

1666

Fire of London.

Death of James Shirley.

1667

Jonathan Swift born.

Milton's *Paradise Lost* published.

Sprat's *The History of the Royal Society* published.

Dryden's *SECRET LOVE.*

1668

Death of D'Avenant.

Dryden made Poet Laureate.

Dryden's *An Essay of Dramatic Poesy* published.

Shadwell's *THE SULLEN LOVERS.*

SHE WOULD IF SHE COULD.

Travels to Constantinople as secretary to the English ambassador to Turkey.

1669

Pepys terminated his diary.

Susannah Centlivre born.

1670

William Congreve born.

Dryden's *THE CONQUEST OF GRANADA,* Part I.

1671

Dorset Garden Theatre (Duke's Company) opened.

Colley Cibber born.

Milton's *Paradise Regained* and *Samson Agonistes* published.

Dryden's *THE CONQUEST OF GRANADA,* Part II.

THE REHEARSAL, by the Duke of Buckingham and others.

Wycherley's *LOVE IN A WOOD.*

Returns to London.

1672

Third Dutch War began (ended 1674).

Joseph Addison born.

Richard Steele born.

Dryden's *MARRIAGE À LA MODE.*

1674

New Drury Lane Theatre (King's Company) opened.

Death of Milton.

Nicholas Rowe born.

Thomas Rymer's *Reflections on Aristotle's Treatise of Poesy* (translation of Rapin) published.

1675

Dryden's *AURENG-ZEBE.*

Wycherley's *THE COUNTRY WIFE.**

1676

Otway's *DON CARLOS.*   *THE MAN OF MODE.*

Shadwell's *THE VIRTUOSO.*

Wycherley's *THE PLAIN DEALER.*

1677

Rymer's *Tragedies of the Last Age Considered* published.

Aphra Behn's *THE ROVER.*

Dryden's *ALL FOR LOVE.*

Lee's *THE RIVAL QUEENS.*

1678

Popish Plot.

George Farquhar born.

Bunyan's *Pilgrim's Progress* (Part I) published.

1679

Exclusion Bill introduced.   Is knighted and marries a "rich old

Death of Thomas Hobbes.   widow."*

Death of Roger Boyle, Earl of Orrery.

Charles Johnson born.

1680

Death of Samuel Butler.

Death of John Wilmot, Earl of Rochester.

Dryden's *THE SPANISH FRIAR.*

Lee's *LUCIUS JUNIUS BRUTUS.*

Otway's *THE ORPHAN.*

1681
Charles II dissolved Parliament at
Oxford.
Dryden's *Absalom and Achitophel*
published.
Tate's adaptation of *KING LEAR*.

1682
The King's and the Duke of York's
Companies merged into the United
Company.
Dryden's *The Medal*, *MacFlecknoe*,
and *Religio Laici* published.
Otway's *VENICE PRESERVED*.

Receives a pension from the Duke
of York, later James II.

1683
Rye House Plot.
Death of Thomas Killigrew.
Crowne's *THE CITY POLI-
TIQUES*.

1685
Death of Charles II; accession of
James II.
Revocation of the Edict of Nantes.
The Duke of Monmouth's Rebel-
lion.
Death of Otway.
John Gay born.
Crowne's *SIR COURTLY NICE*.
Dryden's *ALBION AND ALBAN-
IUS*.

Appointed envoy to Ratisbon by
James II; arrives at Ratisbon in
November.

1687
Death of the Duke of Buckingham.
Dryden's *The Hind and the Panther*
published.
Newton's *Principia* published.

1688
The Revolution.
Alexander Pope born.
Shadwell's *THE SQUIRE OF AL-
SATIA*.

1689
The War of the League of Augsburg
began (ended 1697).
Toleration Act.

Leaves Ratisbon after the accession
of William III; goes to Paris.

Death of Aphra Behn.
Shadwell made Poet Laureate.
Dryden's *DON SEBASTIAN.*
Shadwell's *BURY FAIR.*

1690
Battle of the Boyne.
Locke's *Two Treatises of Government*
and *An Essay Concerning Human
Understanding* published.

1691
Langbaine's *An Account of the English*   Dies in Paris.*
Dramatic Poets published.

1692
Death of Lee.
Death of Shadwell.
Tate made Poet Laureate.

1693
George Lillo born.*
Rymer's *A Short View of Tragedy*
published.
Congeve's *THE OLD BACHELOR.*

1694
Death of Queen Mary.
Southerne's *THE FATAL MAR-
RIAGE.*

1695
Group of actors led by Thomas
Betterton leave Drury Lane and
establish a new company at Lin-
coln's Inn Fields.
Congreve's *LOVE FOR LOVE.*
Southerne's *OROONOKO.*

1696
Cibber's *LOVE'S LAST SHIFT.*
Vanbrugh's *THE RELAPSE.*

1697
Treaty of Ryswick ended the War
of the League of Augsburg.
Charles Macklin born.
Congreve's *THE MOURNING
BRIDE.*

Vanbrugh's *THE PROVOKED WIFE.*

1698

Collier controversy started with the publication of *A Short View of the Immorality and Profaneness of the English Stage.*

1699

Farquhar's *THE CONSTANT COUPLE.*

1700

Death of Dryden.
Blackmore's *Satire against Wit* published.
Congreve's *THE WAY OF THE WORLD.*

1701

Act of Settlement.
War of the Spanish Succession began (ended 1713).
Death of James II.
Rowe's *TAMERLANE.*
Steele's *THE FUNERAL.*

1702

Death of William II; accession of Anne.
The Daily Courant began publication.
Cibber's *SHE WOULD AND SHE WOULD NOT.*

1703

Death of Samuel Pepys.
Rowe's *THE FAIR PENITENT.*

1704

Capture of Gibraltar; Battle of Blenheim.
Defoe's *The Review* began publication (1704–1713).
Swift's *A Tale of a Tub* and *The Battle of the Books* published.
Cibber's *THE CARELESS HUSBAND.*

1705

Haymarket Theatre opened.

Steele's *THE TENDER HUS-BAND.*

1706

Battle of Ramillies.

Farquhar's *THE RECRUITING OFFICER.*

1707

Union of Scotland and England.

Death of Farquhar.

Henry Fielding born.

Farquhar's *THE BEAUX' STRA-TAGEM.*

1708

Downes' *Roscius Anglicanus* published.

1709

Samuel Johnson born.

Rowe's edition of Shakespeare published.

The Tatler began publication (1709–1711).

Centlivre's *THE BUSY BODY.*

1711

Shaftesbury's *Characteristics* published.

The Spectator began publication (1711–1712).

Pope's *An Essay on Criticism* published.

1713

Treaty of Utrecht ended the War of the Spanish Succession.

Addison's *CATO.*

1714

Death of Anne; accession of George I.

Steele became Governor of Drury Lane.

John Rich assumed management of Lincoln's Inn Fields.

Centlivre's *THE WONDER: A WOMAN KEEPS A SECRET.*
Rowe's *JANE SHORE.*

1715
Jacobite Rebellion.
Death of Tate.
Rowe made Poet Laureate.
Death of Wycherley.

1716
Addison's *THE DRUMMER.*

1717
David Garrick born.
Cibber's *THE NON-JUROR.*
Gay, Pope, and Arbuthnot's *THREE HOURS AFTER MARRIAGE.*

1718
Death of Rowe.
Centlivre's *A BOLD STROKE FOR A WIFE.*

1719
Death of Addison.
Defoe's *Robinson Crusoe* published.
Young's *BUSIRIS, KING OF EGYPT.*

1720
South Sea Bubble.
Samuel Foote born.
Steele suspended from the Governorship of Drury Lane (restored 1721).
Little Theatre in the Haymarket opened.
Steele's *The Theatre* (periodical) published.
Hughes' *THE SIEGE OF DAMASCUS.*

1721
Walpole became first Minister.

1722
Steele's *THE CONSCIOUS LOVERS.*

1723
Death of Susannah Centlivre.
Death of D'Urfey.

1725
Pope's edition of Shakespeare published.

1726
Death of Jeremy Collier.
Death of Vanbrugh.
Law's *Unlawfulness of Stage Entertainments* published.
Swift's *Gulliver's Travels* published.

1727
Death of George I; accession of George II.
Death of Sir Isaac Newton.
Arthur Murphy born.

1728
Pope's *The Dunciad* (first version) published.
Cibber's *THE PROVOKED HUSBAND* (expansion of Vanbrugh's fragment *A JOURNEY TO LONDON*).
Gay's *THE BEGGAR'S OPERA*.

1729
Goodman's Fields Theatre opened.
Death of Congreve.
Death of Steele.
Edmund Burke born.

1730
Cibber made Poet Laureate.
Oliver Goldsmith born.
Thomson's *The Seasons* published.
Fielding's *THE AUTHOR'S FARCE; TOM THUMB* (revised as *THE TRAGEDY OF TRAGEDIES*, 1731).

1731
Death of Defoe.
Lillo's *THE LONDON MERCHANT*.

Fielding's *THE GRUB STREET OPERA.*

1732

Covent Garden Theatre opened.

Death of Gay.

George Colman the elder born.

Fielding's *THE COVENT GARDEN TRAGEDY; THE MODERN HUSBAND.*

Charles Johnson's *CAELIA.*

1733

Pope's *An Essay on Man* (Epistles I–III) published (Epistle IV, 1734).

1734

Death of Dennis.

The Prompter began publication (1734–1736).

Theobald's edition of Shakespeare published.

Fielding's *DON QUIXOTE IN ENGLAND.*

1736

Fielding led the "Great Mogul's Company of Comedians" at the Little Theatre in the Haymarket (1736–1737).

Fielding's *PASQUIN.*

Lillo's *FATAL CURIOSITY.*

1737

The Stage Licensing Act.

Dodsley's *THE KING AND THE MILLER OF MANSFIELD.*

Fielding's *THE HISTORICAL REGISTER FOR 1736.*